T0382352

Bello:
hidden talent rediscovered

Bello is a digital only imprint of Pan Macmillan,
established to breathe new life into previously published,
classic books.

At Bello we believe in the timeless power of the imagination,
of good story, narrative and entertainment and we want to use
digital technology to ensure that many more readers
can enjoy these books into the future.

We publish in ebook and Print on Demand formats
to bring these wonderful books to new audiences.

www.panmacmillan.co.uk/bello

Emma Donoghue

Born in Dublin in 1969 and now living in Canada, Emma Donoghue is a writer of fiction, history, and drama for radio, stage and screen. She is best known for her international bestseller *Room*, shortlisted for the Man Booker and Orange Prizes and winner of the Commonwealth (Canada/Caribbean), Rogers Writers' Trust and Hughes & Hughes Irish Novel of the Year Awards. Her fiction ranges from contemporary (*Stir-fry, Hood, Landing, Touchy Subjects*) to historical (*Slammerkin, The Woman Who Gave Birth to Rabbits, Life Mask, The Sealed Letter, Astray*) to fairy-tale (*Kissing the Witch*). For more information, go to www.emmadonoghue.com.

Emma Donoghue

WE ARE
MICHAEL FIELD

First published in 1998 by Absolute Press

This edition published 2014 by Bello
an imprint of Pan Macmillan, a division of Macmillan Publishers Limited
Pan Macmillan, 20 New Wharf Road, London N1 9RR
Basingstoke and Oxford
Associated companies throughout the world

www.panmacmillan.co.uk/bello

ISBN 978-1-4472-7957-0 EPUB
ISBN 978-1-4472-7955-6 HB
ISBN 978-1-4472-7956-3 PB

Copyright © Emma Donoghue 1998

Visit **www.panmacmillan.com** to read more about all our books
and to buy them. You will also find features, author interviews and
news of any author events, and you can sign up for e-newsletters
so that you're always first to hear about our new releases.

Katherine. On the other hand, feminist scholars have occasionally bought into the Michael Fields' own myth that their union as lovers was perfect, with no tensions, no rivalries, no pain. One story-line in the diaries which I had not expected described Edith's tormented passion for their art critic friend, Bernhard Berenson. The Michaels' sexual identities were complicated by the fact that, apart from each other, they much preferred men to women. (And further complicated by their erotic and religious passion for a chow dog.)

The more I found out about Edith and Katherine from their diaries, the more superbly contradictory they became. They were Anglicans, then atheists, then practising Pagans, then Roman Catholics: As fussy Tory spinsters and free-thinking suffragist Aesthetes, they wept for the deaths of both Queen Victoria and Oscar Wilde. Hardworking, witty, generous in love and friendship, they were also bitchy, snobbish and monstrously egotistical. They saw life as a work of art, and faced brutal death as an adventure.

From the middle of the 1970s, a number of literary historians (most notably Henri Locard, Kenneth Ireland, David Moriarty, Jan McDonald, Holly Laird, Yopie Prins and Angela Leighton) have begun to pay the Michaels' poetry and journals the tribute of close reading and intelligent criticism. J. G. Paul Delaney's decades of research on the artist couple who became the Michaels' best friends, Charles Ricketts and Charles Shannon, has added a great deal to our knowledge of Edith and Katherine. What the Michaels deserve and need is a long and thorough critical biography, based on the great treasure trove of unpublished papers, as well as on the full range of their works. However, in the meantime, until someone decides to embark on that Amazonian task, I offer this short and personal study of the intertwined lives of a couple who – both as people and as writers – have come to haunt me.

Many of the Michaels' concerns – how to make history come to life on the page, how to love a woman without marrying her, how to write about sexual passion, how to talk to and about God –

were already mine before I began this book. While I was immersed in their diaries, Katherine and Edith came to seem as real to me as my loved ones. I picked up their vocabulary; I quoted them in every conversation (for which I now apologize to the same loved ones). I experienced a slightly shameful vicarious pleasure from visiting their Aesthetic life: plumed hats, boxes of fresh violets, tours of the Continent, and servants to do all the dirty work. But I learnt a lot from them too: about language, and collaboration, and playing with gender, and courage in times of disaster, and using stamina and imagination to keep love alive. And though Katherine and Edith disliked the Irish, and ended their lives as the most pious Catholics, I suspect they would approve of any book with their name on the cover, even one by a lapsed Catholic Irishwoman.

They were demanding Muses, and some days they drove me mad. (Even their devoted friends sometimes found the Michaels unbearable.) The millions of words Edith and Katherine produced, the excess of their emotions, the energy they poured into every opinion, every encounter, every detail of everyday life – all this can be exhausting. Yet it is that same energy that lights up their work, that makes parts of their diaries sound as if they were written yesterday, that gives this particular pair of ghosts their lasting power to haunt.

A girl

A girl,
Her soul a deep-wave pearl,
Dim, lucent of all lovely mysteries;
A face flowered for heart's ease,
A brow's grace soft as seas
Seen through faint forest trees:
A mouth, the lips apart,
Like aspen-leaflets trembling in the breeze
From her tempestuous heart.
Such: and our souls so knit,
I leave a page half-writ –
The work begun
Will be to heaven's conception done,
If she come to it.

Underneath the Bough (1893)

The spinster aunt

Like many other devotees of Art for Art's Sake, the Michael Fields came from solid bourgeois stock; they, preferred not to remember that their exquisite reveries were funded by cigars.

Katherine Bradley's father Charles came from a respectable Birmingham tobacco-merchant family, but he and his wife Emma Harris were unorthodox in one respect. As Dissenters who were not willing to pay an Anglican priest to unite them, they 'married themselves' (in Katherine's words) by means of public vows on 4 May 1834 along with two other couples, 'untrammelled by law', being 'resolved to mix life's sacraments themselves'. (After a long campaign, Nonconformist and register-office weddings were legalized two years later in 1836, and the Bradleys were considered married by everyone who knew them.) Their decision caused pain to their parents and many local cousins, but Katherine was always proud of Charles and Emma for taking such a stand, even if it left her technically illegitimate.

The couple settled down quietly after that at No. 10, Digbeth, Birmingham, beside the Bradley tobacco factory. Their first daughter, Emma (known as 'Lissie' to distinguish her from her mother) arrived eleven months later on 1 February 1835, and a second, Katherine, eleven years later on 27 October 1846.

Cancer was the family disease. In 1848, it killed Charles Bradley. Katherine was only a toddler, but she claimed later to remember her father as 'noble & bold & true'. Emma Harris Bradley was now a wealthy young widow; she moved to the suburbs and brought up her daughters with the help of a German nurse and a maid called Alice. Katherine later complained that the house had a sombre Nonconformist atmosphere. A friend described Katherine and Lissie's mother at this time: 'she belonged to the prophets & ascetics & held her head like an Empress above her angular, unlovely gowns.'

Katherine was short, healthy looking, with a squarish face and golden hair. She and Lissie both benefited from their mother's belief in a liberal education. Instead of school, they had a series of tutors who taught them French, Italian, German, Classics and painting. For the younger sister, in particular, this policy paid off. Katherine became a lifelong self-educator, fearless in libraries. Theatre was an early passion; her favourite cousin, Francis Brooks, remembered how she used to round up the horde of relatives to perform plays at New Year. Already in childhood she was so addicted to writing poetry that her letters were often in rhyme. As she wrote in her sixties,

FOR LIFE IS SO MIRACULOUS INSIDE
MY BEATING BRAIN, IT WERE A SUICIDE
TO GIVE NO RECORD OF IT TO THE PEN.

The Bradley girls' education was not meant to prepare them for any career but that of wife and mother. Upper-middle-class English Victorian men prided themselves on the 'idleness' of their women; only such genteel pursuits as art, music, literature and charity work were encouraged. The Bradley sisters responded very differently to the future they were offered. As Katherine put it later, Lissie was pragmatic and sensible, free of Katherine's 'terrible intenseness'. As an adolescent, Katherine enjoyed socializing with 'the Brum-folk', as she called her relatives, and caught the train to concerts, lectures and art galleries in London. But she was prey to 'gloomy fits' and was notorious for her deep blushes and her deafening shrieks at times of crisis. The sisters were further divided when Lissie married James Cooper, a businessman seventeen years her senior. Emma

Bradley grew closer to her elder daughter during the engagement, helping her shop and sew her trousseau. 'The wife has to mould her whole nature to her husband's,' Katherine observed later; to her, marriage seemed a risk and a sacrifice. The wedding fell on Katherine's fourteenth birthday in October 1860. She and her mother must have felt lonely, because within the year, when they heard Lissie was pregnant, they began spending long periods with the Coopers in their house in Kenilworth in the West Midlands.

On 12 January 1862 Katherine was walking through a meadow in the moonlight, when James came up to her, shouting, 'There is a dear little baby'. Later, taking her niece into her arms, Katherine burst into tears, but she could have had no idea that this tiny creature, christened Edith, would eventually become the love of her life.

Just over three years later Lissie Cooper gave birth to another daughter, Amy. One of those mysterious after-effects of Victorian childbirth – it could have been spinal damage, a prolapsed uterus or incontinence – was said to have left Lissie perpetually feeble. Certainly she appreciated her mother's and sister's help with the girls. James Cooper was a typical hands-off Victorian father; he sometimes played with the children, but preferred to spend his spare time making elaborate Swiss wood-carvings.

James was an Anglican, and his mother-in-law seems to have given in gracefully and allowed Katherine to worship with the Coopers in the Church of England – the majority faith, and the most socially acceptable. Though Emma Bradley remained a Nonconformist, she occasionally attended Anglican service with her daughters, perhaps as a sop to family harmony. On New Year's Eve 1866, for instance, Katherine felt very proud of her mother, who looked so sunny and handsome compared with the other ladies.

But Mama's brightness covered the usual family secret: cancer. She had known for three years, yet she only told her daughters –

than ever that she was going to meet her Maker, and that death could cause no breach in love. 'I shall be with you, watching over you,' she assured her younger daughter. Katherine finally had to tell the children that Grandma was dying. Edith listened, 'very attentive'; when her aunt mentioned that Grandma liked to hear her voice, Edith went around the house singing. She gathered hawthorn, daisies, and forget-me-nots for the bedside. Throughout her life, she would rely on the language of flowers to an almost obsessive degree.

In the last few days Katherine moved around the house, dusting the ornaments. The terrible to-and-fro ended on 30 May 1868. Seeing her mother's face altered by death, Katherine cried out 'that I was motherless, but my true sister folded me closely in her arms, & promised to be a mother to me always'.

In turn, Katherine had to comfort her white-faced nieces in the garden. Embracing little 'Edie', she reminded her of how much her singing had pleased her Grandma. 'And I sang too,' whispered the three-year-old Amy. Ignoring this, Katherine promised Edith that she would always love her as her Grandma did. 'And you will love me dearly too?' asked Amy. Recording this exchange in her diary, Katherine realized with a mixture of regret and amusement that she had hurt the smaller girl's feelings. But how could she hide such an obvious preference?

The funeral was recorded on the last page of Katherine's diary. Was this a coincidence, or was she already expert at shaping the narrative of her life? Her mother's death was 'the break in the circle'; there seemed to be no one Katherine came first for now. Wondering whether anyone would remember *her* twenty years after her death, she wrote cynically, 'Not unless I have children of my own – nieces will never do it.'

   Her mother left her the country cottage, but Katherine never seems to have lived there, nor did she have much sentimental attachment to Birmingham or its landscape of 'dust & ashes'. From now on, she wrote, she would be homeless, because motherless, 'as a stranger travelling'. And where better to be a self-pitying exile than Paris?

Off she went in October 1868 to study at the Collège de France and to stay with a half-English friend, Miss Gérente. In the Louvre Katherine met a dedicated copyist of illuminated manuscripts. 'She is getting old; looks so happy!!! If I am to be an old maid, I wd fain, fain have such a pursuit; but I have not talent for such devotion.' Katherine's diary – half in French, at this point – shows her fascination with the Gérente family's Catholic rituals and private dramas. In particular, she liked to look at her friend's photographs of her brother Alfred, a startlingly handsome atheist of forty-seven with a mass of dark curls, several children, and an obsessive grief for his musical, bad-tempered, late wife. As soon as Katherine met him, her 'hero worship' ballooned. She could not have chosen a more glamorous and unavailable object for her first experiment in falling in love.

'Oh to be at the bottom of the Seine,' she wrote, enjoying her misery thoroughly. Over the course of a few sociable evenings in 'The Master's' atelier on the Quai d'Anjou. Alfred's mild teasing embarrassed and delighted Katherine: 'I saw, he had been told what I thought of him, & cd not help laughing.' But secretly she thought her passion just might be reciprocated,' and began writing to him. After an evening of wine and *pot-au-feu* and pears, she went home full of dreams of settling in Paris and making him happy at last.

The next morning, 13 November, Alfred was found dead. It was totally inexplicable; all the doctors said was that he had had some sort of 'attack'. Katherine and his sister shared their hysterical grief, watching over the beautiful body of 'a perfect man', though Katherine recorded with irritation that she would have preferred to be alone with him, as her grief was infinitely greater than his sister's. She was now 'sure that he loved me', on the rather feeble evidence that 'he never spoke an ungentle word to me'. She began to write bad poetry about a secret passion: 'Lo, I forget thee not.' At last, life was offering her a story-line to sink her teeth into.

At times, I say, it was awful of God to put such love before me; & snatch it out of my grasp, then I think I cannot praise him enough, for so fully answering my prayer, that I might know the height and depth of human love.

When Alfred's possessions were auctioned, Katherine did not bid for anything, in case people would wonder why she wanted a memento, but for Christmas Miss Gérente gave Katherine a photograph of her brother. 'I can never love any other,' Katherine pronounced confidently at the age of twenty-two; 'I am very happy.'

Her poems about this man she had known for a matter of weeks, and very occasional later references to the anniversary of his death, have been seized on by some historians to explain why Katherine Bradley never married; this is what Lillian Faderman refers to as the 'cherchez l'homme' tactic. Years later, however, Katherine recognized the nonsensical quality of the whole episode: 'Goodness, what a sentimental girl I was.'

Before long she was homesick and returned to Kenilworth. A letter she wrote to James and Lissie thanked them 'for the home they have made & kept for their motherless sister, & the two fair babes they have given her'. In 1873, five years after Mama's death, the family moved to Park House in the town of Solihull outside Birmingham. Lissie was often ill, so Katherine busied herself with 'teaching the chicks'. Amy amused her with bizarre questions such as whether there would be boys in heaven; Edith was quieter and more intelligent. Katherine was still determined to be more than an 'old spinster aunt'. Insisting on some privacy, she shut herself away in the attic in the evenings to write what she later called 'pulpy lyrics'. She kept no diary during these years and we know very little about them; she was treading water.

At last, at the age of twenty-nine, Katherine took the plunge into print. Longman, Green & Co. published her collection *The New Minnesinger* (1875), the title meaning 'singer of love' in German. The pseudonym she chose, 'Arran Leigh', echoed the writer heroine of Elizabeth Barrett Browning's verse novel, *Aurora Leigh* (1857). The collection includes dramatic lyrics to a dead woman, odes to grass, violets, primroses, thrushes and the moon, mildly feminist declarations, religious poems, and translations from Goethe and Schiller. Katherine sent the slim volume by 'Arran Leigh' to just about every bookish man she could think of. Acquaintances wrote back to 'My dear Kittie', and strangers to 'Dear Sir'; already she was enjoying the game of literary androgyny.

But still she hungered for more education. In 1875 she attended a summer course at the newly opened Cambridge college for women, Newnham, where students were encouraged to work on anything that interested them. At first Katherine was terrified of the male professors, and paralysed at the thought of making her maiden speech at the debating society. But Newnham girls lived in a whirl of intense female friendship, and Katherine loved it. Kept away from the male undergraduates for the sake of propriety, few Newnhamites pined; they played hockey, gossiped over their 'work' (sewing), sang, read each other's poems, had daily cocoa parties to make up for the notoriously bad dinners, and held evening dances with one girl in each couple leading, or 'doing gentleman' as they called it. This homosocial world had its own titillating rituals; to 'prop' another girl meant to propose to her that you should address each other by your first names, a delicious mark of intimacy.

The spiritual restlessness hinted at in some of Katherine's early poems now brought her into contact with the controversial ageing giant of the art world, John Ruskin. Desperate for intellectual and religious comrades, Katherine had subscribed to the Guild of St George, a tiny Utopian society founded by Ruskin in 1871. (To prove the glory of manual labour, he had rounded up a group of undergraduates – including a certain Mr O. Wilde – and built a rather bad road outside Oxford.) For two years Katherine and the self-tided 'Master' or 'Tyrant' corresponded on such weighty matters as how to form children's artistic tastes (impossible in England, he told her) and the existence of the Devil. She committed a tenth of her income to his hand-picked charities, and sent violets Amy had picked for him. He wrote from Venice with hints on tailoring for Katherine to pass on to her dressmaker, and urged her to improve her handwriting.

By the time Katherine got to know Ruskin, he was already suffering from bouts of depression and delirious illness which came to dominate his life. He and she often quarrelled – over her hunger for passionate friendship, for instance. 'The next beggar or babe is your "comrade" – and comrade enough,' he told her. Ruskin had stern views on women who talked too much; he called the Irish feminist writer Frances Power Cobbe a 'clattering saucepan'. When Katherine finally dared to tell him that *The New Minnesinger* which she had sent him was her own work, he responded 'how much too serious my life is to be spent in reading poetry', and told her to be grateful he had not thrown it in the bin.

A crisis was inevitable. At Christmas 1877, Katherine wrote to Ruskin in Oxford declaring that the world was so full of evil, she had become an atheist, and took comfort only in her new, squat, long-haired Skye Terrier. In several furious replies he called her a 'goose' and a 'false disciple', comparing her to a child who wanders off the safe road into a ditch and gets gored by wild pigs. Having expelled her from the Guild, he wound up his tirade by claiming that he loved dogs fifty times better than she did.

Katherine's grief-stricken replies softened him, and they were gradually reconciled as she edged back towards a conventional belief in God. But their friendship seems to have petered out around 1880. An undated letter sounds like the last he sent her: Ruskin wrote that 'few whom I have ever cared for at all – have been so little worthy', and Katherine marked this line as 'FALSE' in angry capitals.

Like many another 'serious woman' of her era, Katherine looked to men for intellectual stimulation, however fond she might be of women. She would go on to repeat the pattern of besotted discipleship with several other literary men after Ruskin, but never again would she subordinate herself so completely to a bully. Partly because she was growing up, entering her thirties, but mostly because she no longer needed a 'Master'. She had a 'comrade' instead, her beloved Edith.

Unbosoming

The love that breeds
In my heart for thee!
As the iris is full, brimful of seeds,
And all that it flowered for among the reeds
Is packed in a thousand vermilion-beads
That push, and riot, and squeeze, and clip,
Till they burst the sides of the silver scrip,
And at last we see
What the bloom, with its tremulous, bowery fold
Of zephyr-petal at heart did hold:
So my breast is rent
With the burthen and strain of its great content;
For the summer of fragrance and sighs is dead,
The harvest-secret is burning red,
And I would give thee, after my kind,
The final issues of heart and mind.

Underneath the Bough (1893)

We are closer married

What about Edith? We know very little about the childhood of Katherine Bradley's niece. Though she sounds like a sweet five-year-old child in Katherine's 1867 diary, she seems to have grown into a strange girl. Taken to the coast for her first swim, Edith remembered feeling quite desolate as she stared at the boundless sea. Tall, pretty, pale and narrow-shouldered, with grey eyes, she was even more brilliant than her aunt. She wrote poetry by the age of ten, translated Virgil in her early teens, and liked to puzzle her elders with references to obscure philosophical concepts. (In this she was like one of her cousins, Constance Naden, who went on to become a brilliant linguist, scientist, feminist and poet before dying young.)

Edith's passions were unorthodox from the start: her first crush was on a choirboy with a pale face whom she heard sing a hymn about the Crucifixion, 'Bound up on the accursed tree'. As with Katherine and Lissie in the older generation, Edith had little in common with her sister; little Amy was shy, not noticeably clever, and her chin wobbled whenever she was upset. Only her aunt Katherine really understood Edith; both of them had inherited what Edith called the 'Bradley force'.

They were kindred spirits from Edith's early childhood, but Katherine never seems to have dreamed of finding a life partner in her niece. We cannot tell when or how things changed and they became everything to each other. But by about 1878 – when Katherine, at thirty-two, was exactly twice Edith's age – they were behaving as a couple. Afterwards they claimed that the age gap made them perfectly complementary. In a sense, the two women had no precedents for this relationship; they made it up as they went along. But in another sense they had many different role models, and could call on the rhetoric and conventions of family, friendship, sexual passion and marriage.

Katherine and Edith rarely referred to each other in the cool terms of 'aunt' and 'niece', except in business letters, but their family connection was the rock on which their relationship was built. For many Victorians, family affection was a cult. Passions for parents and siblings expressed in nineteenth-century diaries, which can sound almost incestuous to us, seemed utterly natural to them. 'All love without the blood-tie tortures me,' Edith commented years later; for her, within family was the only space in which the heart could safely open. And none of their family seem to have looked askance at Katherine and Edith's growing passion, woven as it was into the family web of 'darlings' and 'dearests'.

In front of friends they mostly called each other 'my fellow', 'friend' or 'comrade' – rather donnish words with associations of equality and shared work. Romantic friendship – a pair bond between middle- or upper-class women, presumed (sometimes wrongly) to be nonsexual – had been fashionable for centuries in many Western cultures. Though theories about sexual deviance were just beginning to cast their shadows, it was still perfectly possible in the 1870s for respectable, educated women to form long or lifelong domestic partnerships. So common were they in New England that they were known as 'Boston marriages'.

Sisters sometimes formed pairs, and so did cousins; the Irish novelists Edith Somerville and Martin Ross (real name Violet Martin), distant cousins, were romantic friends as well as collaborators. Aunts and nieces paired up occasionally; when Mary Salter Browne died, her niece Alice Maude Browne compiled, printed, bound and distributed a book of letters, photos, pictures and poems called *You and I Together Love* (1906) as a memorial to their relationship.

In tact, a striking number of Victorian women writers had female partners: Eva Gore-Booth lived with Esther Roper, Alice James with Katherine Loring, Sarah Orne Jewett with Annie Fields, Frances Power Cobbe with Mary Lloyd, and Willa Cather with Edith Lewis. We cannot tell how many of them were lovers in a physical sense; what we do know is that their devoted partnerships were socially acceptable. Romantic friends offered each other commitment without a contract, loving company without submission to authority – basically, far more freedom than wives and mothers had.

So when Katherine Bradley and Edith Cooper started socializing as a pair, sleeping together at night and calling each other 'my Love' and 'my Beloved', nobody turned a hair. It was obvious, and quite acceptable, that (as Edith put it) she and her aunt had 'chosen each other with all our strength'. Probably most people assumed that their love was perfectly platonic.

But soon the two were overstepping the boundaries. Their language was much more heated than that of most romantic friends; in poems, Katherine called Edith 'lover'. We do not know when their relationship became sexual; they were too romantic to note it down, because what mattered to them was the love that the sex expressed. And having been together since Edith's birth, they had no need of an anniversary.

Theirs was a particularly interesting transitional lesbian generation, born too late to have full confidence in the innocence of romantic friendship, but too early to feel much need to either hide their love or assert it shamefacedly as 'inverts', like Radclyffe Hall's generation of the 1920s. Edith and Katherine were quite careful about what they said where. They seem never to have dropped hints even to their friends about a physical side to their relationship. In their published poetry, they allowed themselves an astonishing level of sensuality; 'Unbosoming' (at the beginning of this chapter) uses images and rhythms that can only be called orgasmic. But lyric poetry, unlike the more public genres of fiction and theatre, could get away with nearly anything; its story-lines were so much less obvious than those of novels, and therefore easier to turn a blind eye to. Some of their poet contemporaries – Amy Levy, Isa Blagden, Mary Coleridge – were almost as frank about love between women, but the Michael Fields went beyond all their peers in their unashamed evocation of desire.

In the diaries, which they intended should reach the light only long after their deaths, Edith – franker than Katherine – made some rare and vague references to sex. (Nowhere, by the way, did they show any awareness that their love could be considered incestuous; clearly incest only happened between men and women.) It was one of the only things she wrote about briefly and enigmatically, rather than in great detail; the gaps are tantalizing. In April 1892, for instance, she wrote, 'I continue to sleep with my Love, I continue ... to be happy.' In the Scottish Borders in September 1894, she recorded a squabble over a bad dinner, but the next day announced with significant italics, 'we meet, and my poet *meet*.' In March of the following year, she commented, 'My love heals me in her breast,' and in April she recorded that Katherine 'took me to her breast & to young joyousness'. In 1898 she wrote that 'Love-delight has frolicked & throbbed unencumbered & ceaselessly'. In 1904 she announced that this year 'we are each more of a bodily sweetness to each other'. Each of these phrases is open to interpretation, but together they clearly evoke a world of sexual joy.

At no point did Edith use any of the newly available words like 'invert' or 'lesbian' which described – and marginalized – women who loved women. Even when the Michaels turned Catholic late in life and made vows to give up what Edith called 'fleshly sin', they do not seem to have judged themselves harshly as deviants, only as ordinary sinners. One possible explanation of their attitude is suggested by a 1930 autobiography by Mary Casal, who made a fastidious distinction between the sexual 'overindulgence' of the 'real inverts' on the one hand, and, on the other, the 'higher plane' of her own turn-of-the-century lesbian relationship, which included 'sexual intercourse' as an expression of love rather than lust. Perhaps for the Michael Fields, as for Mary Casal, if sex was just one element in a balanced, spiritually enriching love, it did not make you a pervert.

The ideals of Victorian marriage clearly shaped their feelings. Katherine and Edith planned to stay together for life, and did their best always to present a united front, covering up any conflict. But they were careful not to shock friends or family by claiming to be married; they saved that audacious metaphor of union for their private writings. A poem of Katherine's, 'Cowslip-gathering', describes a sort of pagan wedding. The two women, 'twin maiden-spirits', walk hand in hand in the woods. Seeing them so in love, Nature declares 'These children I will straight espouse'. This may refer to the time they first became lovers, but the language is marital. Again, when Edith wanted them to have a home of their own, she referred to it as the opportunity for a 'wedded life'.

In other crucial ways, however, Katherine and Edith were not married, and did not want to be. They were both equally interested in feminine clothes and masculine nicknames; neither had any interest in the polarized roles played with by couples such as Alice B. Toklas and Gertrude Stein, and they would never have dreamed of calling each other 'husband' or 'wife', even as a joke. They kept their finances separate; they had no children. Though they could be possessive of each other, and did not like to spend much time apart, they never quite forgot that they were two individuals, either of whom was free to walk away. Most interestingly, each gave the other a certain license to have feelings for other people, from friendships, through crushes, to (in Edith's case) a grand passion for a man; they saw jealousy as foolish, 'only a defect of sexual life'. Mostly they saw themselves not as loyal spouses but as godlike, untiring lovers. Edith once wrote that the true worship of Eros was impossible for 'mortals who weary of their pleasures in a few thin hours'.

Over a hundred years later, the new ideal of heterosexual partnership or marriage – with separate surnames, bank accounts and jobs, often without children – looks curiously like Edith and Katherine's arrangement of the 1870s. At a time when many gay and lesbian activists are clamouring for the right to legal marriage, it is worth remembering that same-sex lovers have been forming lifelong partnerships for centuries without any need of state or religious sanction.

Katherine and Edith's relationship was not perfect. But it was a strong, evolving organism, with its strategies for compromise and avoiding danger, and its remarkable powers of recovery after quarrels and dry times. Their sense of themselves as uniquely important geniuses made them take their relationship very seriously; they put time, money and thought into it, using holidays, presents and well-timed bunches of flowers to keep the flame burning for the half century they spent together. Ultimately their relationship lasted because of the millions of shared words: through all crises they kept talking, kept writing.

When they began, they had no privacy at all. They learned how to be lovers while surrounded by Lissie and James ('the Old Couple'), Amy, Old Sally the cook and various maids. In 1878, when Katherine was thirty-two and Edith sixteen, they had all moved to Stoke Bishop, a suburb of Bristol. Home was an ugly modern villa, but at least it had woodbine and myrtles outside the windows. Now that Edith was entering adulthood, she and Katherine could seize more freedom, going into public as a pair and walking over the Downs every day to lectures on Classics and Philosophy at University College Bristol. Their leisure reading included Dante, the Elizabethan playwrights (including the collaborators Beaumont and Fletcher), Robert Browning, Gustave Flaubert, Walt Whitman and Christina Rossetti – one of the very few women writers in whom they had any interest. But they both spoke at debates in favour of votes for women, and Katherine was secretary to the Anti-Vivisection Society in Clifton (a Bristol suburb) for almost a decade (feminism and animal rights often went hand in hand in those days). They rejected corsets and crinolines in favour of daringly clinging dresses in arty colours such as peach, gold or green, with hair loosely knotted at the nape of the neck. This was the medieval, Pre-Raphaelite look which would characterize followers of the Aesthetic Movement a few years later.

Friends, trying to describe Katherine and Edith years later, tended to exaggerate their differences. Katherine was generally characterized as the energetic one – healthy, talkative, bossy, quick to banish someone for a petty offence but just as quick to call them back, with old-fashioned manners, 'stout, emphatic, splendid and adventurous in talk'. She had more of a taste for wine than Edith had, and sometimes smoked with gentlemen visitors, which has led some to label her as the butch. Never as healthy as Katherine, Edith was often described along the lines of 'wan and wistful, gentler in manner'; her prettiness and occasional claims of psychic sensitivity meant that she became characterized as the femme, and the follower, both of which are misleading. Edith certainly spoke less than Katherine in public, out of a crippling shyness; 'I grow in the dark,' she said of herself. But she was an excellent listener, an avid questioner, and liked funny stories. Her diaries reveal that behind that delicate face lay a vigorous, judgemental, sometimes scathing mind, with powerful biases and loyalties. What could the other undergraduates have made of this pair? Certain women, found them thrilling. Some young Oxford men were intimidated by their intellect, or put off by the pretentiously archaic language they spoke, and their closeness to each other.

Neither their student friends nor most of their family had any idea that Katherine was 'Arran Leigh', who wrote after lectures every night in her little blue bedroom, trying to shut her ears to her brother-in-law James reading the newspaper aloud in the next room.

Edith, too, had been writing poetry since her early teens – rather ghastly pagan odes full of exclamations like 'Ai, Ai!' and 'Io, Io!', collected after her death in a volume called *Dedicated*. Though these poems have none of Katherine's lyrical charm, they do have a certain drive, an informed passion for the classical world and more than a hint of male homoeroticism. What the first writings of each woman suggest is that the aunt was too sugary, and the niece too melodramatic, but that in combination they could produce something much better. They began writing their first play.

Collaboration is a mysterious business, and Katherine and Edith wanted to keep it that way. Later they claimed that together they formed one poet, with one unified vision. One of the many literary friends who was to beg for an explanation of their collaboration was Havelock Ellis. Katherine described it to him as a sort of flirtatious, angry dance.

> *The work is a perfect mosaic. We cross and interlace like a company of dancing summer flies; if one begins a character, his companion seizes and possesses it; if one conceives a scene or situation, the other corrects, completes, or murderously cuts away ... Let no man think he can put asunder what God has joined.*

Note the masculine pronouns; as writers, they refused to think of themselves as women. Also, listen to the warning behind her wit: invoking the words of the Marriage Service, she reminded Ellis that her and Edith's collaboration (and, by implication, relationship) was a sacred and indissoluble bond which excluded all men.

But Katherine misled Ellis (and other friends) by portraying herself and Edith as constantly huddled over one desk, their pens weaving in and out. The truth was more down-to-earth: they wrote in separate rooms. Some of the plays they would publish as written by both of them were actually by one or the other. Others were planned by one, or both, and shaped together; they would write long passages separately, each doing the kind of scenes she did best, and then swap them for editing. Their poems they wrote as individuals, though they acted as editors and advisors for each other. They would go on to publish them in joint collections, without even hinting to readers which of them had written which poems.

For their first collaboration, Edith simply added a pseudonym of her own to Katherine's. In 1881, as 'Arran and Isla Leigh', they published a volume of poetry on classical themes, including a four-act play, *Bellerophôn*, named after the slave who rode Pegasus. Verse drama, sometimes known as closet drama, was an ancient form, written for private reading rather than performance. It was fashionable in the nineteenth century: Lord Byron, Percy Bysshe Shelley, both Robert and Elizabeth Barrett Browning, Algernon Swinburne, Matthew Arnold, Arthur Clough and Thomas Hardy all tried their hands at it. The Victorian stage, with its plot-dominated melodramas and low farces, seemed to have nothing to offer the poet who was interested in character and personal vision. Verse drama did offer writers many freedoms: they could break all the conventional rules of theatre, set their plays in any time and place, use as many characters as they liked without having to worry about costumes or fees, and make them do just about anything without fear of the censors or the audience's reaction. The problem was that it cut them off from the excitements and. challenges of the stage, and doomed them to a small and élite literary audience. In beginning their career with *Bellerophôn*, Katherine and Edith had chosen a side, committing themselves to 'the love of art for art's sake', in the famous phrase from the art critic Walter Pater's *The Renaissance* (1873).

Bellerophôn, the first of their historical tragedies, set the Shakespearean pattern: at least three acts, blank verse for the important characters, prose dialogue for the lowlier ones, and some stock types such as the mystical Fool and the loyal Page – to which Edith and Katherine added the prophetic Hag. The best thing about this first, rather undistinguished play is a hag who declares herself unique in her love for her own sex:

WOMEN ARE TO ME
TRUMPETS OF FLESH; I AM THEIR PROPHET, SEER;
I LOVE THEM AS A KING HIS COURTIERS LOVES.
I FILL THEIR EARS, I TIP THEIR TONGUES; O QUEEN, I
LOVE THEM MORE THAN MISER LOVES HIS GOLD.

This volume by 'Arran and Isla Leigh' got little critical attention. Therefore, like a rock group which keeps changing its name to shake off its reputation, three years later, in 1884, Katherine and Edith chose themselves a brand new pseudonym to mark the fusion of their talents: Michael Field. 'Field', with all its associations of nature and open spaces, is said to come from a childhood nickname of Edith's, and 'Michael' may come from the archangel. In an age when male pronouns were considered generic, and femininity and ambition were widely considered incompatible, adopting a man's name seemed the best way for a woman writer to get her work noticed and to be taken seriously as a speaker on universal themes.

But the mask was for Katherine and Edith as much as for the world. In a sense they did want to be men – or at least not mere women. Theirs was a feminism that tried to shrug off gender. When they saw the French actress Sarah Bernhardt in a breeches role, for instance, they recorded approvingly that 'sex is forgotten as an accident – and the ideal lover remains.' In dress they both tended towards the lacy, but in conversation and writing they both liked to butch up. Over the years Edith called Katherine 'Michael', 'Mick', 'Sim' or 'S' (from Simiorg, a fabulous wise Eastern bird), 'the all-wise bird or fowl', and even (slightly tongue in cheek) 'Master'. Katherine called Edith 'Field', 'the Blue Bird', 'the Persian' (cat), 'Puss', 'Pussie', or 'P', and later 'my Boy', 'Henry', 'Hennery', 'Henny', and 'Hennie-boy'. Cross-gendered and animal nicknames were not uncommon at this time; the upper layer of British society has always enjoyed a certain P.G. Wodehouse silliness. But Katherine and Edith took it farther than most, even sporadically referring to each other as 'he', a habit which does not seem to have bothered any of their friends, many of whom played along.

The new joint pseudonym also hid the fact that there were two writers involved. Collaboration was extremely common at the end of the nineteenth century, especially among pairs of men or women, but it was thought to smack of amateurism, and generally only one name ended up on the title page, for fear of reviewers. An 1892 essay by Walter Besant admitted that there were certain advantages to collaboration, especially in the shaping of a play, but argued that 'To touch on the deeper things one must be alone'. Without explicitly advising collaborative writers to lie, Besant did hint that the readers would only be troubled by collaboration if they knew about it: 'We must hear – or think we hear – one voice.'

And he did very well, this newly-invented male playwright, Mr Michael Field, when he burst on the literary scene in May 1884 with a pair of verse plays, *Callirrhoë* and *Fair Rosamund*, published in London and Clifton in a six-shilling volume. *Callirrhoë* – another of their unpronounceable titles – is a stirring four-act tragedy based on an obscure Greek legend. The heroine's brother Emathion is exposed as a snivelling weakling when he fails to offer his life for his sister's. Demophile, the nurse who would gladly die for her beloved girl, tells him with wonderful bluntness, 'I never liked you, and today I think you're nothing but offal.' As for the young heroine, she cannot bear the thought of dying without having experienced pleasure in her body, 'the very love it's fashioned for, / As firebrand for the flame-tip'. But as well as her desire for the priest of Dionysus, Callirrhoë has a very sensual friendship with Nephele. When she finds Nephele dead she does not shrink from kissing her mouth, explaining that 'Love and the vultures are the only things / Death cannot sicken'. This first 'Michael Field' play establishes a world of polymorphous passions, in which desire is never really wrong. As the priest of Dionysus tells his beloved:

LOVE IS THE FRENZY THAT UNFOLDS OURSELVES;
BEFORE IT SEIZE US WE ARE IGNORANT
OF OUR OWN POWER AS REED-BED OF THE PIPE.

Fair Rosamund is less ambitious but more moving. Rosamund –
Henry Plantagenet's mistress, hidden away in a bower in a wood
– is the first of many *femmes fatales* given sympathetic treatment
in Michael Field plays. Henry's wrathful wife Queen Elinor is
another of their wonderful hags; there are great scenes of her
mocking and threatening her husband.

I'LL SHATTER YOU
AS NATURE SHATTERS – YOU AS IMPOTENT
AS THE UPROOTED TREE TO LASH THE EARTH . . .

The unknown Mr Field's first volume got rave reviews; he was
compared to everyone from Shakespeare to Swinburne. Only the
book's local publisher, J. Baker, knew who the author was; he sent
a horseman to tell Misses Bradley and Cooper that the *Spectator*
had announced 'the ring of a new voice, which is likely to be heard
far and wide among the English-speaking peoples'. Katherine and
Edith saved all the clippings and printed four pages of them as a
preface to their next collection of plays, adding gloatingly '*And
numerous lengthy and favourable reviews in other Journals.*'

Flushed with confidence, they began to think of themselves as
professional authors. Congratulations arrived from minor men of
letters such as Marc-André Raffalovich, who sent a long and highly
personal overture of friendship. 'Mr Field' wrote a charming, teasing
reply; Katherine and Edith were convinced that they could enjoy
their persona's fame without risking their own privacy. They failed
in this by accident, through their friendship with a much more
famous mentor, Robert Browning. A widower with a snowy beard,
Browning was not just a poet but a cultural institution. When he
probed for more information about the collaboration, Edith
answered:

My Aunt and I work together after the fashion of Beaumont and Fletcher ... She has lived with me, taught me, encouraged me and joined me to her poetic life ... This happy union of two in work and aspiration is sheltered and expressed by 'Michael Field'. Please regard him as the author.

She made Browning swear 'strict secrecy'. He meant well, but unfortunately he thought the secret was simply their collaboration, not their gender. *Callirrhoë* having sold out, a second edition appeared in November 1884, when a review in the *Athenaeum* referred to the playwright as 'she'. Only Browning could have spread the gossip. Katherine wrote reproachfully to him to explain that they needed a male disguise to let them write freely, escape 'drawing-room conventionalities', and receive honest and fair criticism: 'we have many things to say that the world will not tolerate from a woman's lips.'

Edith managed to make peace between her 'Father Poet' Browning and her 'fellow', and a deep friendship developed. But the damage was done; it gradually became an open secret in literary circles that Michael Field was a woman, or, worse still, two women. Marc-Andre Raffalovich wrote in distress on 16 November to say 'I thought I was writing to a boy'; if he had had any idea Michael Field was a lady, he insisted, he would never have taken such liberties. This letter shows just why Edith and Katherine would have wanted to meet their peers wearing a masculine mask.

But they stuck to the name, though it had lost much of its anonymity. Even years later, when they heard that the art critic Vernon Lee (real name Violet Paget) was gossiping about their true identities, they wrote to her crossly: surely she of all people, with her masculine pseudonym, should understand that 'belief in the unity of M.F. is absolutely necessary' and that 'public reference to him should be masculine'? For years it continued to trouble them that readers might hear that the authors were female and plural, and be put off.

In 1885 the Michael Fields published three new plays. *The Father's Tragedy* was begun by Edith at about sixteen, inspired by Walter Scott's version of the clash between Robert III of Scotland and his son, the Duke of Ramsay. All Katherine contributed was a song. This powerful drama shows the burning idealism of its young author, but also a lot of sympathy for the bewildered elders. 'Nothing glorious / Is marketable', spits young Ramsay as his father's courtiers plot to marry him off to an heiress. (Living on inherited wealth, Edith and Katherine could afford to despise materialism.) The play attacks the power of fathers and arranged marriages – almost as relevant to spinsters in 1880s Bristol as in medieval Scotland. There is a heartbreaking scene in which the imprisoned and starving Duke of Ramsay shrinks back into childhood, and is breastfed by the armourer's wife, who has just lost a baby.

Along with this play they published one of their earliest, a five-act tragedy about Henry VI of Germany set in twelfth-century Italy, called *Loyalty or Love*? Its convoluted story, reminiscent of *Othello*, is enlivened by some good Shakespearean insults: 'you fat flesh-heap', one woman screams at another.

Unlike their other plays, *William Rufus* has no women characters at all. The Earth is the nearest thing to a heroine in this tale of an arrogant king who appropriates the common land, and is killed by an arrow that bounces off an oak tree into his heart: There are some wonderful speeches by the old blind man Beowulf, who addresses Nature like a lover as he mourns a grandson hanged for killing a royal deer.

> FOR NOW HE'S DEAD THE EARTH WILL THINK ON HIM
> AS SHE UNWEAVES HIS BODY BIT BY BIT.
> SHE'LL HAVE TIME LIKE THE WOMEN-FOLK AT WORK
> TO TURN ALL OVER IN HER MIND, AND GET
> HIS WRONGS BY HEART.

The relevance of this play to the Land Question raging in the 1880s – especially in Ireland, where the peasants were demanding a stake in the fields they tilled – shows that the Michaels often disguised political issues in the robes of historical drama. The reviewer for the *Athenaeum* – who was obviously out of touch with literary gossip – thought Mr Field's *William Rufus* an 'essentially virile composition', the writing almost reaching 'the strength of Elizabethan men'. Years later a theatre manager wanted to put it on, but could not find enough good male actors.

In 1886 the Michaels published a play called *Brutus Ultor*, with a preface addressed 'To the People of England', to inspire them to uphold justice. The justice in question is rough: Brutus must order the execution of his traitor sons, and Lucretia must kill herself after denouncing her brother-in-law for raping her. This powerfully written but rather repellent play was their first and last experiment in literature for the masses, or 'the Demos' as Katherine called them, because as well as appearing in hardback, *Brutus Ultor* was also issued as a small paper-covered booklet costing only ninepence. It was ironic that the play Edith and Katherine hoped would capture the hearts and ninepences of the plain people of England was their first real failure, in reviews and in sales.

Katherine and Edith had spent most of the summer of 1885 in Norfolk on their own, sailing on the silent Broads. Searching for a story to express that landscape, they asked Professor A. W. Ward for a subject from Viking history, and he suggested King Canute ... They threw themselves into a tragedy in four acts called *Canute the Great*, in which almost every character's name begins with E, which adds to the confusions of the violent plot. Gunhild the Norse witch and seer is one of their more memorable hag figures. But the best character is the scheming Queen Emma, twice the age of her husband's rival, Canute, but determined to win his love. There is also an extraordinary scene of mutual comfort between Edmund's wife Elgiva and his sister Edith, when their lives have fallen apart through various murders and insanities. Elgiva stops Edith from killing herself, and finds her own consolation in consoling:

I FILL WITH TENDERNESS; GOD SENDS HER
TO KEEP MY HEART A MOTHER'S. HOW IT THROES
AGAINST HER NESTLING FOREHEAD!

Edith, rocked in Elgiva's lap, reverts to childlike happiness: 'I have never / Known all this joy since I was three years old.' They plan to live as sisters in a convent; 'My woman-child, my own', Elgiva calls Edith. It is ironic that this scene, which of all their dramatic work sounds most reminiscent of the Michaels' own relationship, can only happen when one of the women has gone mad. Lunacy lets characters break out of the traditional dramatic story-lines of marriage, birth and death.

In their diaries, on the other hand, the Michael Fields felt able to make their own love the central plot. On 16 May 1886, for instance, they were moved to tears by Browning's stories about his dead wife Elizabeth, and Katherine wrote afterwards,

*Oh! love. I give thanks for my Persian: those two
poets, man and wife, wrote alone; each wrote, but
did not bless or quicken one another at their work;
we are closer married.*

Such audacity, to rate her and Edith's romance higher than that of the Brownings, the famous benchmark of marital passion! Katherine's two verbs, 'bless' and 'quicken' (to become pregnant), are highly sexual. They suggest that the Michaels' personal and professional collaboration was fertile in several senses.

They were travelling more and more these days, partly for inspiration and research, partly for Edith's health, but also to escape from the crowded family home in Bristol. Staying in lodgings near a forest or a beach, they relished their privacy both as lovers and as writers.

On 31 January 1887, Edith wrote to Lissie from Scotland, apologizing for not being there on her birthday: 'oh, darling, you are mother and friend in one – the two most beautiful bonds are twisted together between us.' This was not just gush; though Lissie was stubborn and set in her ways, she was proving a good friend to the poet-couple, and read everything they wrote closely. The same letter sent only perfunctory love to 'Father' (James) and 'my sweet & only sis' (Amy).

Despite being so wrapped up in each other, the Michaels were busy making new friends. One was Arthur Symons, a critic and poet of the Decadent school with sad eyes, a drooping moustache and floppy dark hair. He wrote to a friend to boast that he had visited Michael Field, 'the mystery of whose personality I am not permitted to reveal'. Another new friend was Havelock Ellis, a Socialist in his late twenties, living with his sisters, researching medicine and reviewing theological books for a living, as well as finding time to write a novel. The Michaels also got to know his favourite sister Louie; she used to buy and make clothes for them. Edith generally hated writing letters, but she did correspond regularly with a dear friend called Alice Trusted. Robert Browning, or 'the Old' as they called him, remained the Michaels' most important mentor. 'N.B. The "Old" likes caraway cake', Edith noted for future reference after one tea-party. Katherine was forty-one and he was seventy-five, but she still found him utterly seductive. As she told Edith in a letter, 'Truly, love, I would fain put back the clock thirty years, and be loved by Robert Browning in his glorious manhood.' The fact that she could share such a fantasy shows that the women's love felt too secure to be threatened.

Their next play, *The Cup of Water*, is a pastoral tragedy about the right to love, and much easier to follow than most of their others. Though it begins like a classic Tudor play about honour – what should a man do when he and his friend fall in love with the same woman? – it comes to the startling conclusion that fulfilment would be better than renunciation. Cara is one of the Michaels' most intriguing heroines. Adolescent, utterly uneducated, she has a powerful bluntness. Hearing that the young king she loves is already engaged to a princess, she says 'Great ladies cannot love./You must be poor and famished to be hungry.' The play argues for the forces of nature against fossilized conventions and promises:

BONDS SENSELESS AS THE WINTER COVENANT
OF FROST-BOUND FOREST THAT, AT RISE OF SAP,
BREAKS INTO RED AND OLIVE.

It is strongly feminist in its emphasis on how wrong it is for men to decide women's fates without consulting them. It can also be read as a coded plea from its lesbian authors for readers to respect 'the holy law of perfect, human passion', no matter how unusual or disruptive that passion may be. But of course the high-minded sacrifice is made and half a dozen lives get ruined; God forbid the Michael Fields should write a happy ending.

Canute the Great and *The Cup of Water* appeared in 1887, bound in vellum at seven and six, and did not attract very much attention. Several of their friends, noting that most reviewers knew enough to call Michael Field 'she' these days, became gradually convinced that sexist bias was working against the two writers. Certainly, it would seem just too much of a coincidence if, despite their writing better plays, their reputation just happened to decline around the same time as their gender came to be known.

They could not have kept going without the support of their intimates. Edith's sister Amy loved reading drafts of their work to her friends, and the Michaels were gathering quite a fan club who had great fun playing with their pseudonym. Katherine's cousin Francis Brooks wrote to the 'Dear Sacred Ones' and signed himself 'Michaelian', as if Katherine and Edith were the twin deities of a cult he had joined.

In their last year at Bristol, 1887, there was a time of 'chaos' which they referred to only vaguely in later diaries with phrases like 'the stormy romance' or 'the old love-tragedy'. Francis Brooks fell in love with Katherine. Years later, Edith described a typical evening: Lissie sewing, James listening to Chopin, and Francis sitting opposite Katherine, 'taking the music as the expression of his youthful passion'. He may have proposed; we have no reason to believe that she gave him any reason to hope, but James Cooper, possessive of his houseful of women, locked horns with the younger man anyway. Edith, who often alluded to this time in her later diaries, never sounded at all jealous or resentful; clearly Francis was not a serious rival.

Partly in an effort to escape 'the poison of the last year' there, the Cooper ménage decided to move south in 1888. Browning urged his 'two dear Greek women' to come and live in London, near him, but instead the family settled in 20 Blackberry Lodge, Reigate, Surrey, about thirty miles due south of London. Francis Brooks was shattered by their departure, and always held a grudge against James, but remained deeply fond of both Katherine and Edith. In Reigate the Michaels could enjoy quiet country living but reach London easily by rail, especially as some trains went faster in those days than a century later; they thought nothing of popping up for an evening to see a play. Lissie and James had separate rooms in Reigate; so did Katherine and Edith, but they always slept together in one or other of them, which did not trouble anyone.

The Michaels were shedding many of the Bradley and Cooper values they had inherited. Somehow they managed to reconcile their Anglicanism with a new worship of the colourful pagan deities evoked in their plays; they built an altar to Dionysus in the garden and said prayers such as 'I salute the Earth & the home of the gods above'. As Katherine told Havelock Ellis, 'I am Christian, pagan, pantheist, and other things the name of which I do not know.'

They began to keep a joint journal, proudly tided 'Works and

Days'. Unlike their famous predecessors, the brothers Edmond and Jules de Goncourt, who wrote with one voice, the Michaels made separate entries – Edith in a deft scrawl, Kathenne in a schoolgirlish loopy script. They took turns to write it up in retrospect, every few days, often from their joint notes; this allowed them to shape petty details into a grand narrative. There were to be no secrets. Katherine and Edith used the diary to tell each other painful things as well as to reassure; if one was away, the other would read and write in the diary as a sort of psychic phonecall. Sometimes there were gaps of months, but they never lost the habit till the end of their lives, which makes 'Works and Days' – thirty tall creamy leatherbound ledgers – a unique document of a writing life. Everything found its way in: letters, uplifting Bible quotes for New Year's Day, picture postcards, notes on paintings, occasional tallies of money owed each other, transcripts of conversations with literary men, bad jokes and limericks, lists of books borrowed from Mudie's Lending Library, garden reports, book contracts, scandalous newspaper clippings, obituaries, invitations to art shows, and a long conclusion (with New Year's resolutions) at the end of each year. In the British Library's Manuscript Room, the reader turns a brittle page and a pressed flower falls out, a souvenir of some walk the lovers took and wanted to remember, still bright yellow after more than a century.

Their new project was *Long Ago*, a collection of lyrics inspired by the poetry of Sappho of Lesbos (sixth century BC) – mostly fragmentary half-lines, said to be all that was left after the Church burnt the rest. Obviously the Michaels were drawn to Sappho as a way of writing about lesbian love at a safe distance, 'long ago'. But this sophisticated sequence of sixty-eight poems deals with many different passions, overlapping along a spectrum of sexuality, much like Sappho's own work. Browning was immensely enthusiastic about this collection by his 'two dear Greek women', as he called them. When on a visit of 9 May 1888 they asked him to write a preface, he told them they did not need his endorsement. They recorded his advice proudly: 'We must remember we are Michael

Field.' Speaking of their neglect by the critics, he advised them, 'Wait fifty years.'

Long Ago contains fourteen poems about Sappho's unrequited love for Phaon the boatman, and several about the young poet Akaeus's unrequited love for her. Other poems dramatize the pleasures of daily life, moon worship, weddings, and Sappho as insomniac watching her pupils sleep. Against the backdrop of this tender affection for girls are set a handful of impressive poems which evoke physical passion between women. In Poem XXVII, where the repulsive Gyrinna is contrasted with lovely Mnasidica, the speaker's unabashed gaze is on her breasts:

> BUT WHEN MNASIDICA DOTH RAISE
> HER ARM TO FEED THE LAMP I GAZE
>   GLAD AT THE LOVELY CURVE;
> AND WHEN HER PITCHER AT THE SPRING
> SHE FILLS, I WATCH HER TRESSES SWERVE
> AND DRIP, THEN PAUSE TO SEE HER WRING
> HER HAIR, AND BACK THE BRIGHT DROPS FLING.

Sometimes there is a strong hint of voyeurism, as in Poem XXXV:

> COME, GORGO, PUT THE RUG IN PLACE,
>   AND PASSIONATE RECLINE;
> I LOVE TO SEE THEE IN THY GRACE,
>   DARK, VIRULENT, DIVINE.

What saves this collection from sentimentality is the knowledge that betrayal and loss are unavoidable: 'those whom I love most give me pain', as Sappho concludes in Poem XXVII. Danger is all around in Poem XIV, based on a tiny fragment of Sappho's which mentions dawn as a queen:

> ATTHIS, MY DARLING, THOU DID'ST STRAY
> A FEW FEET TO THE RUSHY BED,

WHEN A GREAT FEAR AND PASSION SHOOK
MY HEART LEST HAPLY THOU WERT DEAD;
IT GREW SO STILL ABOUT THE BROOK,
AS IF A SOUL WERE DRAWN AWAY.

ANON THY CLEAR EYES, SILVER-BLUE,
SHONE THROUGH THE TAMARISK-BRANCHES FINE;
TO PLUCK ME IRIS THOU HAD'ST SPRUNG
THROUGH GALINGALE AND CELANDINE;
AWAY, AWAY, THE FLOWERS I FLUNG
AND THEE DOWN TO MY BREAST I DREW.

MY DARLING! NAY, OUR VERY BREATH
NOR LIGHT NOR DARKNESS SHALL DIVIDE;
QUEEN DAWN SHALL FIND US ON ONE BED,
NOR MUST THOU FLUTTER FROM MY SIDE
AN INSTANT, LEST I FEEL THE DREAD,
AT THIS, THE IMMANENCE OF DEATH.

In the somewhat more mundane world of Reigate, Lissie was dying
of the family illness – cancer – at the age of fifty-four. The spring
of 1889 was a difficult period for her grieving sister and daughter.
For the first time in 'Works and Days' we read of a 'reckless quarrel'
between Edith and Katherine, and then a 'calm, penitent walk to
Wray Park Common'. But Lissie, like her mother Emma Harris
Bradley, planned to make a good death. It was as if they were all
on a spiritual retreat together – reading, meditating, talking of the
past, or playing with Piano the puppy.

On 23 May, *Long Ago* arrived, a beautiful pale yellow book, with
a medal of Sappho smiling in gold on the cover, and the poems
printed with the English in black, the Greek fragments in gold. It
cost ten and six, and only a hundred copies were printed. Edith
found it odd to be so happy in the middle of grief: 'the pain and
the joy – like weft & woof.' The famous novelist and poet George
Meredith wrote to them to say he had not been so moved by poetry

in years; and although he had recently heard that there were two of them, theirs was 'a voice of one heart'. It was a controversial book. One critic thought it 'a ludicrous and lamentable attempt' to mimic the great Sappho, whereas a four-page review in the *Academy* announced that with this glorious book Michael Field had advanced from apprentice to master.

Charles Baudelaire and Algernon Swinburne were just two of the male writers who had got into trouble for writing poems about lesbian love. But only one reviewer of *Long Ago*, in the *Spectator*, hinted at 'the sinister associations which came to be connected with her [Sappho's] name'. Other reviewers behaved as if they had never heard of these 'sinister associations', and whether attacking or praising *Long Ago*, they tended not to quote from or comment on the more explicit poems of love between women. For once, being ladies – and assumed therefore to be pure-minded – seems to have worked to the Michaels' advantage.

By 20 June, when this tiny edition had sold out, Lissie and her family were making plans for her funeral. 'When I came in from the garden,' wrote Edith, 'she & Sim [Katherine] were talking of the Immortal Life.' One day, when Amy was lying down with an 'attack of pain', Edith persuaded Lissie to come and be nursed in 'our room', promising that yes, she and Katherine would both continue to sleep in it after her death.

So for a while Lissie's sickness drew her into Katherine and Edith's intimacy, renaming her 'Our Darling' and 'the Mother-One', and James was left to sleep alone for the first time in his married life, because sickness was women's domain. Despite her heart attacks and bad dreams from the morphine, Lissie enjoyed the simple pleasures of what she called her 'Indian summer'. Kissing Edith goodnight, one evening, she, murmured 'My Eldest ... my first Love', which suggests that neither her second daughter nor her husband James could compare. Amy, well aware of this, only felt worthy to kiss her dying mother's feet.

Browning. 'We never wrote a song, without thinking how he would react to it ... it will half-kill our poetry.' On the last day of the year they went to his funeral in Westminster Abbey, where violets and lilac covered his coffin. What this year of losses taught them was that pain deepened the capacity for joy. 'I think perhaps the sole road to happiness,' wrote Katherine, 'is by the breaking heart.'

'Love rises up some days'

Love rises up some days
From a blue couch of light
      Upon the summer sky;
He wakes, and waking plays
With beams and dewdrops white;
His laugh is like the summer rain,
      And patters through his voice;
He is so lovely, tolerant, and sane,
      That the heart questions why
It doth not, every hour it beats, rejoice.

Yet sometimes Love awakes
On a black, hellish bed,
      And rises up as hate:
He drinks the hurtful lakes,
He joys to toss and spread
Sparkles of pitchy, rankling flame,
He joys to play with death;
But when we look on him he is the same
      Quaint child we blest of late,
And every word that once he said he saith.

Underneath the Bough (1893)

Poets and Lovers

With Lissie gone, the family became a yoking of two incompatible pairs. James, the crotchety silver-haired widower, and Amy, his pious daughter (on the brink of joining the Quakers, with her hair back in a severe coil), were increasingly marginal to Edith and Katherine's shared life. The Michaels came into their own as 'poets and lovers' now, edging away from the family and spending more time in London.

On day-trips they took notes on the Old Masters in the National Gallery and newer paintings by the Pre-Raphaelites. They saw *A Midsummer Night's Dream* and admired the exquisite programme by the designer Selwyn Image. They bought candles for 'the little Blue Room where we retire from the censuring sounds of our neighbours' music'; clearly even Surrey was too noisy for them. Though the Michaels occasionally met women who were lesbian or bisexual – such as the poet Mary Robinson – they never sought them out, and seem to have preferred the company of men, especially gay men. One new friend was the art historian and man of letters Walter Pater; they used to drop in to his Kensington rooms on Mondays at five, and learned to call him 'Tottie'. At soirees the Michaels could be hard to please; 'no one interesting or companionable was there', they noted after tea at Lady Seton's. They recorded literary gossip in their diary, but 'I always feel to grow shallow listening to these sorts of things,' wrote Edith after one party. Acquaintances were easy to find, but true friends – 'we of the word made flesh' – were rarer.

All their pain about Lissie's death went into *The Tragic Mary*. Mary Queen of Scots is one of their most likeable heroines, but the seeds of her tragedy are shown to lie in her own character. As the first of the Michael Fields' many queens in captivity, she stands for courage in the face of political exploitation and male brutality. Oscar Wilde, at that time a prose writer who had not yet found success in the theatre, wrote to congratulate the Michaels on making Mary much 'closer to flesh and blood' than other writers. Selwyn Image agreed to design them a cover full of crowns and thistles. The book was printed on handmade paper at seven and six, with a large format edition bound in vellum for twenty-one shillings; by now the Michaels had accepted that their audience was small and élite.

The critic Lionel Johnson reviewed *The Tragic Mary* quite positively for the *Academy*; they found his comments on their over-the-top style both 'helpful and distressing'. But the reviewer in the *Athenaeum* bared his claws: 'Some of these things are only extravagant, others approach insanity.' (It says something for the proud defiance of which Edith and Katherine were capable that they included this painful quote in the reviews at the back of their next book.)

In June they set off to the Continent. Edith's first Channel crossing was 'a gentle nightmare'; she lay rigid in her bunk. In Paris they took the unusual step of visiting the Morgue; they were both so impressed that they named it 'Michael's church'. Edith wrote afterwards that it had nearly killed her to look at death 'unflinchingly', but that more wisdom was to be found there than in the Cathedral of Notre Dame.

They mixed with other ex-pats such as the society hostess Mrs Chandler Moulton. On 9 June they were about to leave a party of hers when she urged them to stay 'to see a beautiful boy'. Amused by this, the Michaels lingered and met Bernhard Berenson, a twenty-five-year-old Lithuanian-American art expert. Edith found BB (as his friends called him) 'packed with ideas as a pomegranate with its seeds'; both women were struck by his sultry good looks. His visits to them in Paris aroused the jealousy of their literary friend Arthur Symons, who seems to have had rather a crush on Edith. Trying to make themselves worthy of BB's conversation, typically after a visit to the Louvre the Michaels would fill six pages of their diary with notes on paintings. They moved on to Milan, Florence, Verona, Bologna, Pisa, Genoa ... the diary for the next six weeks was almost all notes on art.

Back in Reigate, things felt flat. On 21 July they went to another 'at home' at Mrs Chandler Moulton's in London, but she could not resist showing off, and introduced them to the whole party 'as a poet, as Michael Field'. Katherine recorded their rage:

> *We stood, our wings vibrating in revolt fashionable women lisped their enchantment at meeting with us. A moment came when this could be borne no longer. I laid a master-hand on the hostess, and told her to introduce us by our Christian names.*

Feeling so at odds with their sex, the Michaels sound in this passage like another species altogether – masterly archangels, forced to hobnob with silly mortals. But they relaxed as soon as the men arrived; the Irish novelist George Moore gave them detailed praise of their work, and they met Oscar Wilde, who engaged them in a wonderful discussion about the English language's deficit of words for colour. They could not resist hinting to Wilde that they were Michael Field; part of them longed for the publicity that the other part shunned.

James Cooper was now seventy-two, a retired businessman who wanted a comfortable home and all his womenfolk round him. In July, without consulting them, he bought a house in Reigate called Durdans. 'A home on the earth, – a sacred acre our very own,' wrote Edith with relief. Durdans was an ordinary, modern villa, with an exceptional garden that had endless roses, creepers, a rockery and some half-tame field mice. They first went to see it at twilight, and Amy read aloud from St John's Gospel.

By the end of the summer, the Michaels had become fervent self-appointed disciples to BB, much as Katherine had been to Ruskin more than a decade before. They saw Berenson as such an authority that they addressed their letters to 'Dear Doctrine'. By contrast, Berenson called himself 'The Faun', after the character he loved in their play *Callirrhoë*. Privately, he did not think much of their other writings, but relished their company and enthusiasm for art: 'you who can enjoy so much', he called them. George Moore became a proper friend of theirs this summer too. On 30 August he visited Durdans in his 'red stockings and shapely boots'. Though they found him too Irish – meaning tactless and dissolute – they very much enjoyed discussing stagecraft with an expert. He urged them to think about entrances and exits and to avoid the 'haphazard development of plot'; he was convinced that they could write for the stage.

They had launched into a new play about the Holy Roman Emperor Otto III. Immersed in research, Edith observed in her diary on 24 August that women needed to create, one way or another: 'They must be mothers in body or brain . . . The child or the Poem!' As ever, their characters formed a substitute family for the Michaels: children, siblings, lovers even. They invested in these fictional people the time and passion they did not give to James and Amy. When Katherine found terrible remarks about Otto in a book in the British Library, she came home crying on the train. When Edith had to write the part about Otto's death, she felt so 'stricken' that her doctor was worried about her.

Winter, with its cold and lack of flowers, was always a trial to the Michaels, but they found plenty of entertainment. On Guy Fawkes Night they went through a gorgeous frost to see the fireworks on Reigate Heath, with people dressed as devils silhouetted against the flames of the giant bonfire. At Christmas they played Blind

Man's Buff, Egg and Spoon and Forfeits; Katherine read aloud from Charles Dickens' *The Pickwick Papers*. She and Edith still missed Lissie, of course, but they felt so much more alive this year; they were enjoying being a couple, off on their own.

Décor was crucially important to the Michaels; after the purchase of a new cream-painted bookcase for Durdans, 'we vowed a vow to exclude all dark wood from our honeysuckle-bower'. On Good Friday 1891 Edith was completely distracted from contemplation of the Crucifixion by fabric patterns. The Michaels often recorded their worries over money in their diary, but theirs were the tensions and problems of the rich: how to afford all the beautiful things they wanted and still spend their summers abroad. On one occasion they were driving to Shoreditch in London to collect the perfect sofa, they passed hordes of 'sad, mis-shaped, mis-featured work-people'; the tone was that of travellers on safari.

In February Katherine was invited back to Cambridge by the Principal of Newnham College, Miss Clough (sister of the poet). The 'dear, green scum' in the ditches made Katherine very nostalgic for the summer she had spent there in 1875, as did the debates, concerts, dances and kisses from old friends. The same Professor Sedgwick she used to fear now called 'to pay homage' to one half of Michael Field. She had tea with a circle of students, 'selfconscious damsels', who insisted that she decide which of them was the prettiest. That night she knelt under the stars in her narrow room and thanked God for the transformation in her life over those sixteen years: 'I return a poet and possessing a Poet.'

Another literary friend of this time was the critic Lionel Johnson, an Oxford Aesthete in 'girlish shoes and blue silk stockings'; he had a forehead as domed as the British Library Reading Room, they noted, and just as full of scholarship. With the poet Dollie Radford and her husband they gossiped about the suicide of Amy Levy. (Levy, whose poetry makes her passion for women fairly clear, had committed suicide at twenty-eight by inhaling charcoal fumes; what the Michaels never mentioned was that she was a perfect example of what could happen to a lesbian who wasn't lucky enough to find and keep a 'beloved'.) Constance Wilde's dresses took up many lines in their diary – as did Oscar's outfit on 17 June 1891, when he wore 'a lilac shirt and heliotrope tie'. Beatrix Potter (in her pre-*Peter Rabbit* days) offered them cigarettes 'in manly fashion', and, after they refused in shock, smoked one herself. Katherine and Edith both liked the occasional private cigarette, but would never have dreamed of being so unladylike as to smoke in public.

They stayed in close contact with Bernhard Berenson and got to know his 'constant companion', a remarkable woman called Mary Costelloe (nee Pearsall Smith), a freethinking American feminist, daughter to a Quaker preacher woman. Mary had an Irish barrister husband and two small children, but never let that slow her down. Katherine and Edith also met her literary brother, Logan Pearsall Smith, an 'Oxonian gentleman amateur' as they noted slyly. In March 1891 they lunched at Mary's place in London. 'My Love [Katherine] looked Dionysic in red-wine-coloured velvet under her radiant face,' wrote Edith in their diary. Intellectually stimulating as well as charming, Mary Costelloe could have been the close female friend the Michaels lacked, but for the one person who came between them: BB.

Mary's parents had a house near Haslemere, south-west of Reigate. The parties she gathered there were famously Bohemian. In a black cape and red fez, she ran to greet Katherine and Edith at the station when they arrived on 20 May. There were picnics among the beeches and cowslips, nights sleeping by the campfire, and earnest talk of Socialism and Anarchism. At first Edith was distressed by the large group, but it was worth it to be with BB: 'Gaily Bernie and I stray off together – for I lose all shyness as soon as I am in téte-à-tête.' She and Katherine had developed a strange habit of telepathically 'willing' to make things happen, but it did not always work. When they visited BB in London later they coveted a picture of him in his youth, but he remained psychically deaf and never thought to offer it.

They now planned a great trip to the Continent, ostensibly for art's sake – BB had given them a list of paintings to see – but mostly to meet him and Mary in Dresden. The Michaels set off on 6 August, to Belgium, then Germany, and at first it was a successful pilgrimage. At Aachen, they knelt at the tomb of Emperor Otto, hero of their tragedy, and Edith surreptitiously kissed it when the verger had turned his back. In Dresden she felt 'intolerably, disgracefully ill' but simply gargled with eau-de-Cologne. They went to see enough paintings to fill nearly forty pages of the diary; they particularly loved Giorgione's luscious *The Sleeping Venus*.

Edith was not just tired, however; she had come down with scarlet fever. In the coach on their way to the hospital, 'We clasp each other with an awful weight of anxiety on our hearts, for they may strive to part us and we have no German with which to plead.' Katherine used French to beg to be let into the hospital, despite the danger of catching the fever herself: '*O Monsieur, on ne craint pas quant on aime*' ('Oh sir, nothing frightens those who love'). The kind doctor wrote her down as a fever-sufferer also, which let her in the door. She immediately threw a tantrum and demanded a bigger room and good food and wine for Edith.

Katherine lay on her single bed in the moonlight and talked of their travels while Edith slipped deeper into delirium. As Edith wrote later, in a fascinating stream-of-consciousness journal of her fever, 'I beg my Love to keep a candle lighted to put out the moon with all its terrible spectral frilliness and to obliterate the white cavern-arch of the door – Death's Door –'. She conceived a hatred for an ugly nurse, 'the Mädchen'. Her fantasies were influenced by an essay she had been writing on Botticelli's painting *Venus and Mars:*

> *I determine I will have as much pleasure as I can. I dance at balls, I go to Operas, I am Mars and, looking across at Sim's little bed, I realise that she is a goddess, hidden in her hair – Venus. Yet I cannot reach her … I grew wilder for pleasure and madder against the ugly Mädchen. Sim comes to quiet me and assure me she is 'The Little Horse'.*

Katherine immediately ordered the Mädchen out of the room for coughing.

Quite apart from the fact that Edith nearly died, this hospital stay was an experience neither would ever forget. BB and Mary visited five times over a few days; they brought peaches, grapes and pink roses that sent Edith into 'an insatiable rapture'. Another unnamed nurse, known in the diary as Sister or Schwester, cut Edith's hair off – customary when convalescing after fever – and nicknamed her 'Heinrich'; Katherine soon Anglicized this to 'Henry'. Edith was depressed by the haircut, but then realized she had a new androgynous charm to go with her new name: 'she looks very pretty in her short boy's hair & fresh cotton jacket,' she wrote of herself.

Martha Vicinus's essay on 'The Adolescent Boy: Fin de Siècle Femme Fatale?' points out that for the Decadent generation of the 1890s, even for such atypical writers as the Michael Fields, the boy represented a unique combination of pre-heterosexual innocence and spiritual purity on the one hand, and liberty and erotic adventure on the other. (In particular, this generation adored the boy who was really a woman in leggings, from the popular genres of music hall and pantomime to loftier forms such as opera and Shakespearean drama.) Many lesbians, according to Vicinus, used the figure of the boy, the not-quite-man, as a symbol for their difference. It was in the hospital at Dresden that Katherine discovered the flirtatious androgyne in Edith, and for the rest of their lives she referred tenderly to her 'Henry' or 'Hennie-boy' with a variety of male names and pronouns.

She was not the only one to feel this attraction. Schwester, a stern, unglamorous woman in four pairs of stockings and strong boots, who claimed to have no ties on the earth except for her patients (her 'children') and Jesus, was falling in love with Edith. 'While I am away,' recorded Katherine,

P[ussie] drinks 'Kaffee' with Sister for an hour. Sister kisses her with a kiss that plunges down among the wraps (Yes, as the wolf did when he sought the child – O Eros! – in Browning's Ivan Ivanovitch *– a fatal kiss.)*

Katherine's remarks, despite the playful animal metaphors, show a certain anxiety. But she did not feel left out for long: 'My Love & I have our first Springtide kisses – sweet & brief & full of the future. Pussie feels his cheeks reclaimed by love.' This being August, 'Springtide' must have meant Edith's convalescence. Edith added mischievously in brackets, playing them off against each other,

My Love was a little jealous, stormily tearful that nurse should have forestalled her on my lips ... the motherliness in the wonderful passion of Nurse's gave me delight ...

But Katherine was too mature to be threatened by such a lonely old woman; her jealousy was swallowed up in compassion. 'Poor old Schwester' loved Edith, she wrote, like a dog would, or a desert traveller finding an oasis. At one point Katherine tactfully went into the garden to watch the fish, leaving Schwester to more grasping and kissing and cries of '*Ich bin so hungrig*' ('I am so hungry'). Edith had to give her a little slap on the cheek to make her stop, then a kiss on the lips to comfort her.

For all her flippancy and sophistication, Edith seems to have felt a little nervous of Schwester, who at one point threw herself on Edith, kissing her on the mouth and breast, with the *fearful passion of unsatisfied senses in a strange nature, to whom religion has been an ascetic law ... She makes me shiver, but I play with her passion like a child and she is utterly deceived in it herself.*

When Edith finally told her that 'she grieves and fatigues me', Schwester did try to control herself until Edith left the hospital.

My experiences with nurse are painful – she is under the possession of terrible fleshly love she does not conceive as such, and as such I will not receive it.

The Dresden diaries are feverish and often contradictory. Was it just Schwester whose 'fleshly love' was so 'terrible' (because it was frenzied and unreciprocated), or did Edith and Katherine ever feel haunted by the darker side of 'Eros' in their own lives too? Was physical love a simple human need, or a wolfish monster, as it was portrayed in some of their plays?

The diary provides no answers, but it shows that the Dresden episode gave the Michaels new erotic roles to play. 'My Pretty Boy wants to get up,' wrote Katherine, and a month later, 'P[uss]. sleeps all night in its new, winter, fur-lined mantle!' Despite Edith's weakness they continued their trip; she lay haggard in a lace dress on the floor of the Sistine Chapel to look at Michelangelo's Madonna, and often spared a thought for Schwester's loneliness.

Back in Reigate in October, she found it hard to adjust to a daughterly role again after the summer of 'liberty from father'. On Katherine's birthday, which was also James's wedding anniversary, he put the dampener on things by acting the grim widower, and the roast was a disaster. But Edith and Katherine enjoyed the day anyway, and decided to entertain the maids with the story of St Sebastian's martyrdom.

In early December Edith had a dream: she was at a tea party which turned into some kind of religious drama, with BB playing Dionysus and everyone else singing. Katherine leapt up to shout, 'Edith, don't you sing.' But Edith sang on. Here we have the basic elements of the crisis happening in the back of her mind: BB as the deity of a cult, asking a response of Edith which Katherine was trying to block. After knowing BB for a year and a half, Edith's feelings for him were getting a little out of hand.

It was the family's first Christmas at Durdans, and the first with a turkey (as Lissie had preferred chicken). Edith turned thirty on 12 January 1892; she and Katherine breakfasted at a new little table in their study on 'a noble clawlike group of bananas', looking at photographs of Old Masters, then went out and fed the swans, despite the thin layer of snow. They missed Lissie, but Edith was beginning to acknowledge that 'the Mother one' had never understood or set her free the way Katherine did, 'who loves me & whom I love with strenuous force, that is half-hidden by our caresses & humorous names, & utter familiarity'.

One day in spring, Katherine headed for the capital but Edith had to stay at home with James: 'I am shut up as a nurse to an influenza patient who never smiles & who talks platitudes – poor father,' she added, to sweeten the remark. On other days the Michaels caught the train together, with their valises monogrammed M.F., and stayed at the University Club, 'our little Bond Street home'. This was a quiet base where they could rest, write in their diary, and take notes on paintings. They were looking rather frumpy on 25 May when they rushed through the rain to a party, where Oscar Wilde shook hands with them without saying a word, and they felt dreadfully snubbed. Not that Oscar was beautiful himself: 'There is no charm in his elephantine body tightly stuffed into his clothes,' Edith wrote vengefully.

Katherine was staying with her friend Amy Bell on Valentine's Day, and Edith pined all morning. 'I am away from my own identity,' she told their joint diary; 'I want & want ... my own Love, &

nothing else.' But after an hour of 'futile pen-scratching' she got down to work, and wrote a long speech all in one go. Edith seems to have written best when left on her own, and on some level, instinctively, they both knew that. Though they claimed that parting was agony, they quite often chose to be parted; as lovers as well as writers, they found short absences refreshing.

They went to a traditional family wedding in Birmingham after Easter. They no longer felt a part of the 'Brum-folk'; 'How much closer to me are my readers than my relations,' wrote Katherine wryly. The only one they were glad to see among fifteen cousins was dear Francis with his 'unhappy, faithful smile'. They bitched about how ugly and forward the bride was, and how the boys wore 'unnatural lavender trousers'. More seriously, Edith wrote down her doubts about marriage: it was an ancient rite, yes, but it needed 'new forms or new freedoms' to renew it. After champagne and speeches, she concluded 'Ugh! But the cake is excellent.' The previous winter, their friend Havelock Ellis had married Edith Lees out of mutual 'comradeship'; the couple went halves on the cost of her ring and maintained separate lives. (What the Michaels did not record in their diary, if they knew it, was that he had soon found out that his wife was a lesbian.) ' "Free love, free field" is sacreder' than such a mockery of marriage, Edith wrote after a visit from Havelock. 'Free field' suggests the open spaces of a relationship untouched by the state, as well as a pun on her own nickname. So neither the traditional form of marriage nor the unromantic Ellis version pleased her – nor did any partnership, it seems, except hers and Katherine's.

On 23 April, Edith saw Katherine off on a brief trip to Dover. Perhaps vows were still very much on their minds from the wedding, because there in the noisy, steamy station, they made one of their solemn promises – which Katherine gave permanence to in a poem called 'Prologue' as soon as she could sit down in the carriage and get her pen and ink out.

IT WAS DEEP APRIL, AND THE MORN
SHAKESPEARE WAS BORN;
THE WORLD WAS ON US, PRESSING SORE;
MY LOVE AND I TOOK HANDS AND SWORE,
AGAINST THE WORLD, TO BE
POETS AND LOVERS EVERMORE

'Lovers' is a very unusual word in Victorian women's poetry, but what is really startling here is the combination of 'poets and lovers' swearing a reciprocal passion, in a Western poetic tradition in which the (male) poet usually addresses the (female) beloved. The poem ends with the speakers vowing 'to dwell / indifferent to heaven and hell'. As Angela Leighton has pointed out, the poem contains several echoes of Charles Baudelaire's 1857 poem 'Lesbos' about Sappho, named as lover and poet: '*Et l'amour se rira de l'Enfer et du del*' (literally, 'And love will laugh at Hell and Heaven.')

Amy had been in San Remo in Italy with a group of Quakers; her pious letters were full of the Quaker pronouns 'thee' and 'thou'. But in May 1892 she had some kind of breakdown, became alienated from the community – to her family's quiet relief – and came home. 'Dr Sturge speaks of break-up of the nerves – remedies: massage & a winter in Egypt,' Edith recorded wryly. Unable to afford such a trip, James sent his daughter to the London suburb of Shepherd's Bush, for a sort of rest cure in a 'dingy' house with a very large masseuse.

Her sister and aunt were going through the usual pre-publication tension for their book of poems based on paintings, *Sight and Song*. Katherine knew she was nagging their new publisher Elkin Matthews ('The Elk') with her endless queries, but it was worth it when the 400 copies appeared with a simple olive cover and a lovely frontispiece by Selwyn Image. The picture poem was a popular genre; Charles and Mary Lamb, Robert Southey and Leigh Hunt had all tried it earlier in the century. The paintings behind *Sight and Song* are mostly oils, and all by Italian Old Masters, with the

for one special man. The Michaels decided that it would be too embarrassing to explain why they wanted to go home early; instead, they would become more independent. They dined glumly on their own from now on, and Edith spent her days recording every smouldering or uncomprehending glance between her and BB.

Desperate to get some artistic education, at least, the Michaels finally offered to pay Berenson for his commentary on paintings. After the first manly rejection of the idea, he gave in and let them pay him per class; Edith was so ashamed for him. On some level at least BB was aware of her feelings: 'Miss Cooper & I should marry – & be miserable ever after,' he joked cruelly. But she had to admit he was right: 'the fascination we have for each other makes us wretched.' She was projecting her feelings onto him here; we have no reason to believe that Berenson's liking for Edith ever went so far as to make him wretched.

By July they were all irritable. Mary and Edith were both ill, and BB had somehow given himself a black eye on a pile of books. Crossing a street, Edith rushed in front of an omnibus, and Katherine scolded her so severely that Edith accused her of gnashing her teeth. The quarrel, as usual, was recorded self-mockingly in the diary. It was time to go home.

Back in Surrey they felt unlikeable, unsure about art, 'every feather plucked from our wings'. Once Mary and BB came back to London, the Michaels continued to hover around them; although they referred to BB as 'a poor little parasite', they could not break the link. Katherine worried for Edith, and (for the first time in the diary) expressed some fear that an outsider could break their magic circle: 'O Henry, Henry, my Boy, let us cleave to art.'

Edith took the opportunity to answer this while Katherine was away in Oxford: 'Let her not fear,' she wrote. Though BB enthralled her, she had no intention of running 'off to the hills' (more a symbolic than a literal elopement) – partly because it would damage her art, but mostly because she knew how lucky she was to have Katherine. 'There is no fellowship, no caress, no tight winding-together of two natures, no tenderness when my Love is severed from me.' Later she told a friend that BB was her 'twin soul', too like her to make her happy, whereas Katherine was her complementary 'lover soul'.

As a writer of tragedies, Edith could only see her crush in the most histrionic of terms. She continued to report on 'the torture of love' for BB every few months over the following years. But these declarations grew less and less convincing. Life went on, and most days she was happy. From late 1892 on her feelings for BB seem to have had as little effect on her daily life as toothache might, or a longing for gin.

As ever, the Michaels used their pain as the raw material for literature. Edith wrote a series of lyrics in which a woman speaks of and to a man, with tides like 'I Live in the World for His Sake'. The speaker asks the Creator why she and her man friend are 'two souls forbidden to draw near'. At the end of one poem, set in the Luxembourg Gardens in Paris, the singular speaker becomes plural, and concludes 'we twain have given our heart / To him, we are his forever'. This was a very imaginative way of rewriting the fact that one of them was in love with a man. Edith and Katherine were each other's 'poets and lovers' still, for all they had been through.

Constancy

I love her with the seasons, with the winds,
As the stars worship, as anemones
Shudder in secret for the sun, as bees
Buzz round an open flower: in all kinds
My love is perfect, and in each she finds
Herself the goal: then why, intent to teaze
And rob her delicate spirit of its ease,
Hastes she to range me with inconstant minds?
If she should die, if I were left at large
On earth without her – I, on earth, the same
Quick mortal with a thousand cries, her spell
She fears would break. And I confront the charge
As sorrowing, and as careless of my fame
As Christ intact before the infidel.

Underneath the Bough (1893)

Works and days

At heart, the Michael Fields were career women. For the rest of the 1890s, they would live through family crises, professional disasters and the most important friendship of their lives. But nothing halted the flow of writing for more than a few weeks; they were impressively productive. Sometimes a new project would distract them from an old one half-way through – 'each play its own temptation', as Katherine wrote ruefully, admitting that she and Edith were as promiscuous in their worklife as they were faithful in love. But they continued to publish on average a play a year, as well as volumes of poetry, through good times and bad.

For years they had been working on their tragedy about Emperor Otto III, but when it was published, *Stephania* (1892) turned out to be a revelation of women's anger. Set in Rome in 1002, its heroine is an Emperor's young widow, gang-raped by the soldiers of his usurper, Otto. Unlike the heroine of *Brutus Ultor* who kills herself as a point of honour after being raped. Stephania gradually decides to survive, and to turn the weapon of sex back on those who used it against her.

> I WAS TOO WEAK AT FIRST TO APPREHEND
> THE MYSTERIES BEYOND THE KNOWLEDGE FORCED
> UPON ME, AND I WANDERED 'MONG THE HILLS
> FOR SOLITUDE: THEN SLOWLY IN MY HEART
> THERE SWELLED THE PRESSURE OF A SECRET JOY
> AS IN THEIR MAGIC FOUNTAINS I BEHELD
> MY FORM STILL BEAUTIFUL, AND RECOGNIZED

She becomes a famous courtesan, all the time plotting to seduce and murder Otto, who allowed his soldiers to rape her.

Otto is one of the Michael Fields' well-meaning but tragic kings. There is much homoerotic caressing between him and his tutor Gerbert, who is the third character in this 'dialogue'. Stephania charms them both and then plays them off against each other. 'She unveils her dazzling breast with a scornful laugh', reads one stage direction. Maddening Otto with sex, she then kills him with slow poison, and ends the play unpunished and unrepentant. It is possible that this play is partly a fantasy of revenge on BB for the way he had played with and manipulated their friendship.

Imperial Rome and 1890s London, Edith wrote, were very similar in 'laxity – wealthy – degeneration'. The Michaels knew just how outrageous they were being in their attack on corruption, in making a heroine of a prostitute murderess. 'Does he fear, does he sicken over our morality?' Edith asked herself after a gloomy meeting with their publisher, Elkin Matthews. The play was published in November, 250 copies on handmade paper with dove-grey covers and a frontispiece of nuts and leaves by Selwyn Image; the Michaels' meagre fee was thirteen free copies.

Stephania is one of their best plays; with just three strong characters and a clear, painful plot it keeps the reader gripped and moved throughout. But literary men did not get the point. Though he read it three times for its poetry, their friend George Meredith found he still sympathized more with Otto than Stephania, which Edith recorded in her diary as 'a curious pt. of view'. Reviews were late, few and all too often echoed Meredith's point of view. Katherine wrote to a friend, identifying it as a feminist play and pleading with her to use her influence to get it reviewed:

It is a woman's book, & women must defend it. Except a
few dusty old cousins, all my women friends rejoice in Stephania
... Men of course don't like this.

Patriarchy had its tensions at home in Reigate too James and his
sister-in-law often 'jar & excite each other', Edith noted regretfully.
In early 1893 the quarrels came to a head one evening when
Katherine came home from hearing Amy lecture in a schoolroom
on Christian Social Union. Edith recorded the appalling row.

Conversation gets high on Socialism with father – a storm
gathers, breaks – a crisis is onus – He says Sim must leave –
I join my hand to hers & go out, not looking at him ... It
is my whole impulse to go with my Love – to sever all other
ties violently and simply – her dismissal is nothing less than
mine, if love is love.

Defiant, Edith told her father to sell Durdans and get a smaller
place with Amy, while she and Katherine would share a flat in
London. For a few hours, she felt exhilarated at the prospect of
such freedom. But James's pathetic reaction – 'you are going to
leave me forever' – and Amy's sobbing dread of having to live
alone with her father, combined to break Edith's resolve. By the
end of the next day they had all agreed to go on as before. Edith
and Katherine had, however, won a crucial point by declaring their
willingness to walk out; no one would ever try to part them again.

The atmosphere of the house continued to crackle. Both the maids,
Emily and Alice, decided to leave; 'I shall miss her pretty shell ears,'
Katherine wrote of Alice. Even the Michaels squabbled, though in
their loving way: 'there in the garden, hand in hand, have our
quarrel out, as we sun ourselves like cats.' A holiday on the coast,
where they lay on the beach burying their hands in the sand like
children, revived their romance: 'They don't know at home that
we are here,' Edith recorded gleefully. Through all the crises of
missed trains and eerie railway hotels they grew closer. Edith made

shadow pictures in the moonlight of werewolves on the bedroom wall to make Katherine laugh.

They decided that Elkin Matthews's limp efforts at promotion were to blame for the rut their career was in, which may have been partly true. They went back to George Bell & Co for their next and most likeable collection, containing four years' worth of poems. *Underneath the Bough: A Book of Verses* (1893) has a yellow cover with gold letters; the endpapers are a glorious seaweed silk. The book includes songs from their plays, many vivid, impressionistic glimpses of nature, poems to the dead, loving odes to unnamed women friends, and a sequence of poems to men (Meredith, Browning, but mostly Edith's poems to BB, which she disliked in retrospect).

'The Third Book of Songs' is a section containing most of Katherine's most extraordinary poems to Edith. Some have the medieval trappings of Pre-Raphaelite paintings. The speaker celebrates the lady's beauty, swears loyalty and laments being parted. But there is no attempt to make the 'knight' sound male, and having a female speaker rejuvenates this tradition. Another original feature is that the beloved is not haughty, but responsive:

> WHO LOVETH HERE NO TUMULT HATH OR PAIN;
> HER CLOUDY EYES ARE FULL OF BLESSED RAIN,
>   A SKY THAT CHERISHETH; HER BREAST
>   IS A SOFT NOOK FOR REST.
>   SHE HATH NO VARYING PLEASURE
>   FOR PASSIONS FITFUL MOOD;
> HER FIRM, SMALL KISSES ARE MY CONSTANT FOOD
> AS ROWAN-BERRIES YIELD THEIR TREASURE
>   TO STARVING BIRDS.

In the context of Victorian poetry, some of these poems are shockingly sensual: 'That girl will learn who dares become a lover', declares one. A poem full of fear, 'If I but dream that thou art gone', ends with confident desire:

> WAKE ME
> WITH THY KISS-WARMED BREATH, AND TAKE ME
> WHERE WE ARE ONE.

The collection has its low points: the inevitable fauns, bumblebees, encounters with fairies, 'ta la la lo' and so forth, as well as the unforgivable couplet, 'Ye lambkins cling / To her, and frolic in the sunshining'. When Katherine wrote a poem as a love-gift to Edith, she treasured it as such; her feelings robbed her of any clear, objective judgement. Luckily, that passion produced some of her most brilliant poetry, as well as some of her most banal. Although Bell had printed only 150 copies of *Underneath the Bough*, because he feared disappointing sales, it soon sold out, and a revised edition was published in the autumn. It is one of the great ironies of the Michaels' literary career that they saw themselves as playwrights first and foremost, but readers generally preferred their poems.

By the middle of April the Michaels were off to Italy again, and immediately unhappy: BB was being 'execrable', Edith noted. They kept no diary for the next two months. In letters to friends, Mary Costelloe described Katherine, with her 'frowsy flowing hair', wearing a huge fur wrap around her neck on the hottest days, claiming that it kept her cool. The locals were mystified by the visitors until Mary spread the word that they were poets – like Dante – which explained everything. 'A friendship like a letter without a signature', was how Katherine described the inconclusive, uncomfortable bond between the two couples.

As soon as Katherine and Edith got home to Reigate, James and Amy headed off to Scotland; Edith and Amy may have been discreetly conspiring to keep Katherine and James apart. The writers were delighted to be working and living according to their own timetable: 'We both like our salmon cooked the same time.' When all four had to share the house, the Michaels worked 'locked in the dining-room late at night', refusing interruption.

Recently the plays of Henrik Ibsen – serious, emotionally convincing, written in relatively naturalistic prose – had been making the Michaels think again about writing a modern prose drama for the stage rather than an ancient poetic one for the page. The story they found in a newspaper could only be considered modern in comparison with their usual gods and warriors. In the Hungarian Rising of 1848, a man called Ferencz Rényi, faced with the unbearable choice of betraying his regiment's whereabouts or seeing his family get shot, lost his memory; his family were shot anyway, and he went mad. *A Question of Memory* is a hardhitting investigation of heroism and the influence – for good or bad – women could have on men.

The Michaels' prose is an interesting attempt at psychological realism, though it lacks the power of their verse. The two best characters in the play are Ferencz's tomboy sister – 'Now for a military funeral,' she cries briskly when she learns she is about to be shot – and Elizabeth, sweet and grave, who sends men out to die with lines such as 'May I never see you again, dearest on earth.' The play comes to a rather radical conclusion in the fourth act, when after all the betrayals, Elizabeth, mad Ferencz (whom she loves), and his friend Stanislaus (who loves her), all end up in a triangle of platonic friendship, making some sort of home together.

A Dutchman called J.T. Grein had founded the non-commercial, high-art Independent Theatre in London in 1891, and was now looking for a serious British play. He offered to put on *A Question of Memory* just once – on 27 October, Katherine's birthday, an excellent omen. Katherine and Edith were scared but immensely excited: 'Now at last we are to speak with living races of men – to give them *ourselves*.' When Grein told a reporter their full names, Katherine pasted the clipping into *Works and Days* and added 'So at last it is all out. But what matter?' At such a moment of confidence, they were content to let the veil slip.

George Meredith invited his 'twin Muses' to dinner to tease them into pruning some archaic words from the dialogue. Meanwhile the Austro-Hungarian costumes, which Katherine and Edith researched in the British Library, were making this 'the dearest performance ever given' at the Independent. The director, Herman de Lange, bluntly demanded that they cut the children's ballet scene. They told him frostily that 'The ballet – as any artist reading the play would recognize immediately – is essential'. (He was not convinced, and they ended up having to pay for the orchestra themselves.)

The Michaels borrowed a friend's rooms in Gray's Inn to be close to the theatre, and sat in on auditions. The first choice for leading man acted as if he had 'a bread poultice on the chest ... He is intolerable and will destroy our play.' Grein wrote to pacify them: the actor was 'a good man, not handsome but make-up does a good deal'. But after meetings and letters of appeal, the ladies managed to get him replaced with an actor they liked, Acton Bond. Two weeks before the performance they tried to eject yet another actress, but Grein told them firmly 'the work cannot be interfered with any more'.

At first Edith, and Katherine loved the sociability of rehearsals and 'brain-struggles' with 'our little Hock' (though, as Edith commented later, actors were 'a *caste* apart', not quite socially acceptable). The problem was that the bad-tempered director De Lange took against the leading man: 'they hate each other', Edith reported breathlessly in her diary. Terrible battles over script changes at the last minute culminated when the actress playing the fiancée burst into the Michaels' rooms at eleven p.m. to protest against her farewell scene being cut. Still, life was so much more exciting here than in Reigate: 'Would that P[ussy] & S[im] could live at Grays Inn for ever & ever!'

Darling Oscar had booked a whole box, but many of their friends seemed mysteriously unavailable on the 27th. The Michaels dressed to the nines to face their public at last: Katherine in a black and coral dress, with a green velveteen opera cloak edged in black fur, and two white flowers; Edith in a beryl green dress with a red opera cloak. After the first act curtain, certain 'young Michaelians' came round to their box to congratulate them, but then the play gradually fell apart. Someone laughed in the anti-climactic fourth act, and the actor playing Stanislaus panicked and left out most of his last speech. No one shouted 'Author' at the end.

'It seems more natural to be dead than alive. We wake to the surprise of finding every morning paper against us' and 'no word, no letter, no visit' from friends. Edith walked bleakly in the British Museum, longing to climb into one of the sarcophagi. In fact, most of the critics were only patronising rather than vicious, but the Michaels had been so keyed up by their first experience of theatre that they were much more vulnerable than usual. They identified with the martyr hero of the play: 'though everything is against us, we are strong, thank Heaven and our race.' They wrote that they would willingly go through it all again, because above all else women needed 'experience of life'.

One hundred and twenty copies of the script had been published before the performance as by 'Michael Field, Author of *Stephanie*', which showed that they were still proud of that other much-slated play. But before the dust had settled they began to rewrite *A Question of Memory* ... 'Let it drop. It is not a good story,' De Lange advised them brutally; 'Who cares about Hungary?' (This suggests that he had hardly been a wholehearted director in the first place.) The rewrite is a disappointing, shorter, safer play, with the rebellious sister and the strange happy ending both cut out.

The Michaels had not been put off writing for the theatre. In their determination to achieve 'modernity', they started a whole series of contemporary prose plays on such hot topics as hereditary madness, living through one's children, and feminism. But modernity in prose was not their forte; few of the planned plays got very far, and the Michaels never did get to hear that cry of 'Author, Author' from a West End audience.

On New Year's Day 1894 they went to a Dante Gabriel Rossetti exhibition and met Will Rothenstein, 'a five-foot materialist with a frenzy for art', as Katherine described him. But he was only a stepping-stone to another friendship, one that was to be of central importance for the rest of their lives. Charles de Sousy Ricketts and Charles Hazlewood Shannon were a couple, both Royal Academy artists and connoisseurs who published *The Dial* ('that mad journal', the Michaels called it), one of the literary magazines that set new standards of beauty for typography, illustration and binding. In 1892 Ricketts had written a 'Dear Sir' fan letter, but the Michaels only got to meet him and his 'fellow' in January 1894 when, 'by express entreaty' from the Michaels, Will Rothenstein introduced them to the 'brothers-in-art', soon known in the Michaels' diaries as 'the sacred ones'.

They were both a little younger than Edith. Ricketts was barely five foot, with hair like a 'dandelion puff and a devilishly pointed beard; he was an oil painter, a sculptor, a designer of books (including several of Wilde's), jewellery, embroidery, stage sets and costume, an inventor of fonts, and an art historian. It was typical of him to be ambidextrous; he drew with his right hand and engraved with his left. Shannon was best known for society portraits in oil, but he specialized in lithographs, mostly of sensuous bare-limbed women with trailing hair; he was tall and golden, much quieter than his 'fellow'. They tended to wear shiny old blue serge suits that got speckled with cigarette ash, preferring to save their money for the truly necessary beauty of flowers, Greek statues, Old Master drawings or Japanese prints. They had met when Ricketts was only sixteen and had never been apart for more than a holiday since. They now lived in Whistler's old pale lemon house in Chelsea with a blue Persian cat and a German housekeeper called Marie. Wilde called it 'the one house in London where you will never be bored'.

'The Artists', as the Michaels called their new friends, had beauty and intellect – which were the two things the Michaels looked for in men. The tone at these Chelsea gatherings, however, could be rather precious: 'One has to be on one's rarest behaviour – for nothing ordinary is expected,' explained Edith. 'Here in this hateful Reigate,' she complained, 'we have no friends & we cannot bind them to us so far away in town.' But at last on 22 May the Artists were persuaded to make the short train journey down to Surrey. Edith quickly realized on this visit how parallel their relationships were: 'These 2 men live & work together & find rest & joy in each other's love just as we do.' Interestingly, she saw herself and Shannon, the quieter ones, as 'Beloveds', while Ricketts and Katherine were the active, vocal 'Lovers'. Amy joined her sister and aunt in dressing up in their finest clothes to please the eyes of the connoisseurs. 'We bid our guests goodnight with a sense we have walked into friendship as deep as moving grass.'

The Michaels noted in their diary for 9 July that Shannon and Ricketts were devoted to Wilde, but the women hoped that the men 'don't imitate their idol in more than conversation'. This probably referred to his risky adventures in the underworld of 'renters'. As a male couple in an era of suspicion and blackmail, Ricketts and Shannon could not afford to use the impassioned language the Michaels did. Ricketts' surviving letters to Shannon tend to start 'Dear Old Chunkey', 'Chubbers', 'My dear old chap', or 'Dear Old Rotter and Soaker'. (One day they were visited by the married but openly homosexual writer John Addington Symonds, who helped Havelock Ellis write his book on *Sexual Inversion*. At some point in the conversation, so the story goes, Symonds began to nag Ricketts to declare himself – 'But you are, aren't you?' – and Ricketts kicked him out of the house.)

'Have you any secrets?' the Painters would ask excitedly on

postcards. They urged the Poets to write more on Roman and Byzantine themes, exploring the transition between pagan and Christian culture. Besides, an ancient palace was the perfect mental escape from suburban Surrey in a cold rainy June: 'Father reads his papers all day by a starved summer hearth.' The Michaels could only hope to 'escape a long story when we visit him' in the sitting-room, as fish might avoid the hook. They had many a 'Blank Holiday', as Katherine punned, and outbreaks of 'Reigate Sickness'.

Katherine wrote a one-act play in blank verse, *Equal Love*, based on a grim Roman story about the 'equal love' of a strange couple, the Emperor Justinian and his wife Theodora. The Empress decides that she must murder her illegitimate son from a previous relationship to safeguard her husband's throne. When Edith, the 'little human typewriter', wrote out a clean copy of the manuscript, they kissed it seven times and sent it to Ellen Terry, hoping that she would star in it. Instead it ended up in Shannon's beautiful Christmas magazine, *The Pageant*.

A new Irish woman friend, 'Lion' Fitzpatrick, gave Edith one of the few prickles of jealousy she ever had over Katherine. 'Lion *worships* Michael & only admits Field,' Edith noted ruefully after a walk, 'so I had plenty of leisure for looking at midsummer.' Two weeks later Edith was less forbearing: ' "Lion" has a passion for my Love – she is rude and ignoring to me & takes caresses off my Love with a liberty that exasperates me.' This only confirmed Edith's dislike of the Irish. (Lion married the following year, and caused no further trouble.)

In her diaries Edith eroticized her greyhaired forty-seven-year-old aunt not in conventional terms, but by giving tiny quirky details of expression and clothes. When they met in London one day, Edith recorded 'the milk-white teeth of my Love – the black brim of her hat, the radiance from her face ... we kiss & are complete'. Katherine's response to Edith's beauty was even more overwhelming. Once she had packed her bag to go up to London for a play, but when she bent to kiss the little face in the fox fur collar she was so staggered by Edith's beauty and 'the love at her lips' that she cancelled her trip.

Their friendship with the Painters sustained them. Ricketts and Shannon would invite them up to a Private View of somebody's paintings; Katherine and Edith would invite them down for some fresh air or send up boxes of flowers. Ricketts' spelling was unique – he claimed to drink 'shampaign' – and he sometimes included miniature drawings in his letters, such as an Aeolian harp with its strings snapping. A great cache of letters remains, mostly from the Painters to the Poets (which suggests the Poets treasured them rather more). On the outside the envelopes usually said 'Miss Bradley' (as a mark of respect to the elder), but on the inside the letters would begin 'Cher maitre', 'Dear Poet', or 'D.P.'. They called the ladies 'Henry' and 'Michael' or even 'you bad, false, humbugging Mike!' These letters were usually signed 'The Painters' or 'The Artists'; on his own, Ricketts might sign himself 'The Sculptor', 'The Modeller', 'The Sage', or even 'The Oyster' or 'The Tomato'. Privately the Michaels called him 'Fay' or 'Fairyman', and referred to him and Shannon as 'The Brothers' or 'The Apple and the Pear'. These silly nicknames had a serious point; the four of them were devising a vocabulary to celebrate the non-marital but complementary roles they all played. Instead of husband and wife, they could be apple and pear.

Early in the New Year of 1895 Mary Costelloe wrote to say that she, BB and her new male lover were all going to try 'life à trois' – 'the most difficult of all combinations', wrote Katherine dubiously. The Michaels expected to hear from BB, but Mary claimed he was too busy to write, which made Katherine finally lose her temper. 'And now I want to tell you & Mary to sail out of our lives as if you were dead,' she wrote to him petulantly. 'Bon voyage. Illusion perdue. Michael.' That night Edith dreamed that she and Katherine were visiting a tomb in Italy; the effigy came to life and by its long lashes she knew it was BB. 'I – can – lend – you – a – pair – of –

scissors', it gasped, and the two women fled. But in fact BB saved their friendship from the scissors by writing back to say he valued Katherine far too much to let her go.

That spring the Michaels went to Italy and stayed quite harmoniously at Bergamo with BB and Mary (whose other man seemed to be out of the picture now). Meanwhile, at home, the Marquess of Queensberry, not known for his spelling, had called his son's lover, Oscar Wilde, a 'somdomite'[sic]. Wilde's suit for libel failed on 5 April 1895; prosecuted in turn, he was found guilty of 'gross indecency' with rent-boys and sentenced to two years hard labour in Reading Gaol. The Michael Fields could have made a great play of this – doomed love and puritanism meeting head-on – if they could have seen the romance in such a grubby story. Ricketts took up smoking for the first time during the trial, claiming later that it 'saved him from going mad under the strain'. Edith referred to Wilde's sentence later as a 'foolish punishment for an odious offense that shd never have been made public'. 'Much talk about Oscar' overshadowed conversations in Bergamo. Katherine told Berenson that the trial was a personal threat to all 'who sing the praise of youth and beauty'. Perhaps she was coming to realize that her poems, like the one by Queensberry's son Lord Alfred Douglas about 'the Love that dare not speak its name' which was read out in court, were open to suspicion.

But when Katherine and Edith visited the famous art critic Vernon Lee, living nearby with her 'bosom-friend' Kit Anstruther Thompson, they did not feel any sense of solidarity. Both Vernon and Kit seemed appallingly mannish in their tailored suits, and their dogs got into a terrible fight, which made the lady visitors flee to a grassy knoll and refuse to come down until the brutes had been chained. The Michaels had their most peaceful few weeks staying in BB's villa (near Mary's) while he was away. There they could wear his dressing-gowns, relish his austere décor, and feel close to him (or their ideal of him) without being confronted by his shortcomings.

As soon as they left Mary's house, she complained to a friend that they had refused to let her open a window the whole time, for fear of draughts.

> *They think they are a Great Poet – unappreciated at present, but certain to be famous and adored in the next generation – and they think that their souls are united and that it is good for them to be together.*

Anything but, in her view. She swore she would never have them to stay again. But as far as the Michaels knew, Mary had very much enjoyed their company. Off they went to Tuscany, Padua and Venice, where a boatman gave Edith seahorses as a remedy for indigestion.

After working on it on and off for six years, the Michaels had finally finished their play about Carloman, a royal consul who gave up wife, child and rank to become a monk, then rebelled against the rules and fled from the monastery. *In the Name of Time* is a confused play about a confused man, but its debates on marriage and relationships are fascinating. Carloman tells his abandoned wife that vows are meaningless, because it is impossible to say 'so I will remain, / Such, and no other'. With an almost Buddhist sensibility, he suggests that

> EARTH'S WISDOM WILL BEGIN
> WHEN ALL RELATIONSHIPS ARE PUT AWAY,
> WITH THEIR DULL PACK OF DUTIES, AND WE LOOK
> CURIOUS, BENIGNANT, WITH A GREAT COMPASSION
> INTO EACH OTHER'S LIVES.

This play shows the Michaels' interest in the ethics of long-term relationships, as well as their growing hunger for a spiritual home. However, they could not find anyone to publish it; by now they had the reputation of being arrogant eccentrics who wrote too much and too oddly.

They went right on to the next play. Reading Gibbon the historian the year before, Edith had come across the story of the Roman Princess Honoria who conceived a mad passion for Attila the Hun. *Attila, My Attila*! was refused by three publishers. In 'our *Eternal-No* Period', as she called it later, Edith felt like a pauper giving birth to an illegitimate child on the roadside. 'All our friends avoid allusion to our art as if it were a dead husband,' Katherine wrote wryly. The Michaels were forced to go back to Elkin Matthews one last time and agree to a humiliating contract which gave him any profits *Attila* might earn. The first copies of the edition of 115 turned up on Katherine's forty-ninth birthday, some in rose, some in sable green.

It is a play about sexual repression, its heroine, 'the New Woman of the fifth century' as they described her catchily, was written with Sarah Bernhardt in mind. Honoria, the Emperor's adolescent sister, must remain an untouchable, deified virgin so that her brother will have no rival for power. 'But am I not to love?' she pleads with her cold mother. By the end of the play, fourteen years on, Honoria has had a child by a slave, seen it killed by her family, and is now locked up in a convent with her cousin, a nun who loves her in a sadistic way. She still dreams of being raped by Attila the Hun, and wants to see her family destroyed: 'When the storm bursts /Let me be in the thunder-cloud!' Despite the melodramatic plot, Honoria's growing madness is credible, and the play has a certain desolate power.

Attila was the first play they had published since the *Question of Memory* disaster; Edith felt as if she was going 'to the block'. Though the Painters loved it, and a few reviews were positive – the *Athenaeum* suggested the Independent Theatre should stage it – other critics got their knives out. Some were shocked by the line 'Damn your eyes' from lady authors; the *Daily Chronicle* called the play an attack on chastity. But in fact this tiny edition of *Attila* did sell out in the end, and Elkin Matthews even made a little profit for himself.

Mary and BB could not hide the fact that they hated the play. Mary wrote that she wished the Michaels could be stretched beside her on the mint and lavender in Italy, but Edith commented in her diary, 'I'd rather lie where Satan did "chained on the burning lake" than stretch myself on mint & lavender with those two.' For the second time that year, Katherine decided to end the friendship, and wrote to Italy to say so. Edith claimed to be relieved, but then told her diary 'my womanhood is dying'; BB had not lost his ability to upset her. 'Curse, curse, curse the man,' wrote Katherine with uncharacteristic jealousy: 'I have seen my fertile land become a desert through him.'

That winter they buried themselves in a new Roman play, *The World at Auction*. As ever, they took sanctuary in the British Library's Reading Room, 'each little busy bee in its cell & the vast hive over him'. Richard Garnett, the catalogue editor, suggested some early Christian characters to add to the play. The only problem with the British Library was the peculiar café where Katherine unwisely chose the plum pudding, 'the oldest thing in the Museum'.

'Life's struggle begins' was Katherine's opening line on New Year's Day 1896; they found life rather 'savourless' without BB's friendship. Days in Chelsea eating chocolate cake with the Artists helped, as did card games with their local friends – 'mad bouts of "Pig" and "Rowdy Old Maid" ' as well as poker, usually played with matches, but once with real money, which gave Edith the shock of realizing she was a born gambler.

But on 8 March Edith was shattered to receive a book from BB, with a note implying that Mary and he were finished with Katherine but still wanted to be friends with Edith. How dared anyone try to drive a wedge between them? 'I almost hate the beloved Love of my life, because she must sever me from the hateful tyrant,' she confessed to their diary. But she did not write back. Inevitably a quarrel blew up between the Michaels over something petty – whether Katherine should publish all three of her sonnets addressed to Christina Rossetti, or just the best two. As usual Edith broke the tension with tears, then they reconciled with 'love-language' during a walk in the country. Next time Katherine was in London, she sent home a fabulous red silk bodice sewn with garnets and aquamarines.

Their dear cousin Francis Brooks came at the end of March – his first visit to their home in the South. Katherine and Edith feared that 'Father's old deadly jealousy' might erupt again, but the visit went well. Francis claimed to have lived through 'ten years of tears', but he seemed to them to have become a delightfully indolent, gossipy bachelor, his life not at all ruined by Katherine having turned him down.

Quarrels continued to erupt that spring. At Easter James added to the tension by insisting they all come into the drawing-room and sing a hymn of his choice, but Katherine refused. 'When I would rejoin her in the study I am locked out,' Edith wrote in anguish. Finally that night Katherine came to bed, 'took me to her breast & to young joyousness'.

James and Amy set off to Italy on 1 June; 'a noble adventure for an old man' of seventy-eight, thought Edith. They rather dreaded his return; as Edith confessed years later, 'sometimes the pain & fear he brought me almost made me long, out of a life-impulse, for his death'. The Michaels escaped to the Continent themselves in August, on a pilgrimage to Bayreuth to see four Wagner operas in a row. The experience was like climbing a vast mountain, they thought; sometimes boring, often gruelling, but well worth it.

Edith was working like a mad thing this year; she found the constant inspiration 'quite alarming'. It caused more fights, of the kind that were so strikingly absent from their collaboration in other years. When Katherine revised Edith's draft of *The World at Auction*, Edith burst into tears, and finally told Katherine 'I would rather have lost an ear or had a nostril split' than see the play changed in that way. Katherine backed off graciously, Edith went back to her first draft, and peace reigned. One sunny November day on Reigate Hill, Edith told Katherine of her relief that she had made the right choice and cut off from BB; having taken sides, she no longer felt 'torn between mm & Michael'.

In 1894 Ricketts had opened a tiny press, 'Hacon & Ricketts at the Sign of the Dial'. Now in 1897 he was ready to publish something of Michael Field's. They decided on a beautiful new edition of their thirteen-year-old play *Fair Rosamund*. Shannon saw to the layout and Ricketts did the woodcut illustrations, embellished the capitals, and designed the cover. Four such perfectionists could not but clash; when the play came out at last, the Michaels were convinced that Fay had made the doves on the cover particularly obese as revenge for a remark Katherine had once made in favour of curves.

From Italy, Mary Costelloe tried to patch up their quarrel with her and BB in her usual stylish fashion by sending an olive branch (quite literally). But Edith sent only a postcard in reply. She and Katherine were off to France, and needed no guides on this trip.

The fields of Senlis in northern France inspired them to work hard on their next play, *Anna Ruina*. A Russian princess, widow of Henri I of France in the twelfth century, Anna is one of the most interesting of the Michaels' *femmes fatales* who are torn between duty and passion. A restless widowed mother, Anna likes to walk through briars, even if her dress gets torn and wet: 'I will tread no more / On paths prepared', she tells her courtiers warningly. She and the divorced Count Raoul snatch their first kiss in a dark fir wood just before a storm. This is a tender and complex portrait of two adults who are wary of pain and disaster but risk all anyway. Raoul tells Anna:

THE STORMS ARE ON US, CHILD,
THE WINTER CLOSE. SUCH HANDFAST AS I TAKE,
DRAWING YOU DOWN INTO MY UTMOST SOUL
THERE TO ABIDE, TO EE INDEED ITS FELLOW,
MAY TAX YOU PAST YOUR STRENGTH. NO MORE ILLUSION,
NO DREAMS BEFORE OR AFTER! WE ARE AGEING;
IT IS NOT SPRING WITH US. WE HAVE NO HOPES,
NO GOAL BUT IN EACH OTHER, AND, O LOVE,
DEATH IS UPON US.

Edith wrote in her diary that she put a lot of her father into Raoul, but the more obvious parallel is with her and Katherine, still passionate at thirty-five and fifty-one respectively. 'Who does the love scenes? ... You get such words in them,' George Moore said enviously when they went to tea. *Anna Ruina* is one of their most moving plays, with its clear narrative line and strong characters, including Raoul's sexy, masochistic former wife Alienor, and the young page Fernando who loves him more loyally than anyone else does. It must end tragically, of course; Raoul will only be able to be close to Anna again when he is a ghost in the woods of her homeland.

This haunting story was to seem prophetic to the Michaels a few months later, when for the first time their quiet family life became a public tragedy, in what the papers called 'The Zermatt Mystery'. James Cooper and his daughter Amy set off to the Alps for a third summer in a row on 1 June 1897. In his brown suit and small brown cap, James, now seventy-nine, looked barely sixty. As usual, Katherine and Edith relished being alone, despite their annoying neighbour who insisted on playing Chopin very loudly. By Midsummer, James Cooper was in a Swiss hotel, toasting Queen Victoria and singing the National Anthem. Edith was a little worried that her father might overdo it this time; on the 23rd, she began a letter telling him not to try any difficult climbs. But at that moment he was buying a new stick and packing his bag for the

Riffel Alp. 'Believe ever in the love of the Old Paps,' said his last letter.

'Am afraid father has met with an accident': that was the first telegram from Amy – sent to Katherine, presumed to be the stronger of the two. The next explained tersely that James had 'Started slightly ahead of us to Riffel – not seen since, everything being done.' 'Not found, official enquiry', added the third.

For two terrible months the Michaels stopped keeping their diary. Telegrams crossed the continent several times a day, and the Michaels went to Switzerland in mid-July. After three weeks, the Secret Police gave up looking. James's family suspected that he had been murdered by Italian navvies: 'might they be flogged & hanged who wd dare do such an infamy', wrote Edith. But eventually they came to accept that sudden death was better than a slow illness in his eighties; 'It is much to think of the dark years spared him – of his glorious translation,' wrote Edith.

Amy was the one who had lost most, but she always put her sister and aunt first. When they got home to Reigate, there was a present from Amy waiting for them – a Bassett hound, Edith's favourite kind of dog. They called him Musico or Music, 'a most dignified sentimental beast'. They immersed themselves in work, and Edith read Sophocles to learn patience, but the mystery of the old man's disappearance still saddened and obsessed them. A famous Alpine climber, Edward Whymper, kept the case open. Katherine and Edith grew very fond of this stout, fussy bachelor, who had got involved out of sheer kindness.

One of the stunning sequence of poems Katherine wrote about James, 'The Forest' (see the end of this chapter), finally came true. His body was found eventually on 25 October, lying with his head on his hand as if were only sleeping at the bottom of the forty-foot precipice he had fallen into. At first the woodman who found him thought he was a chamois. The Michaels had to wait for confirmation in the *Daily Mail*; they pasted the clipping into their diary. They rushed back to Switzerland, where Katherine identified him by his tie, because 'the loved features' had rotted away; she cut clippings of grey hair for his relatives. After his funeral they stayed on and retraced all the possible routes he could have taken up the glacier, despite their 'wounded feet'. At the summit, they exchanged rings, feeling more wedded than ever because of their shared loss.

Edith gradually became convinced that her father had not simply lost his way, but been lured higher and higher by his wife's ghost. In their diaries she and Katherine now transformed this cranky old man, whose company had often irked them, into their hero, the brave deity of a forest cult. He was the 'lover-father', who had made them feel claustrophobic simply because he had adored them as no other man ever would. In this new interpretation of the past, James had not only inspired all the best men in their plays but had never tried to pry the two women apart: 'he ever approved of our love,' Edith told herself, '& has sealed it by his death.' No one understood; postcards from the Painters seemed utterly inadequate, and other friends' mild letters of sympathy were received with resentment.

Edward Whymper visited on 20 December and cheered them up by asking Edith if Katherine had ever been married, as she seemed to have a married manner.

> *Michael & I make our bed shake with laughter at her stories of the young Mr Bradley who died in the Canary Islands – 'You must have noticed I could never bear the mention of a Canary' sobs wicked Michael.*

They were all a little hysterical, these days. At Christmas dinner Eva the housemaid started crying for the dead Master and then 'went entirely out of her mind'; both she and the other maid Annie left shortly afterwards.

On 26 January 1898 an early birthday present arrived for Edith from their old Bristol friends, the Sturges: a rather wild three-month-old Chinese chow puppy with long red-gold hair. The Michaels immediately named him Whym Chow – after Edward Whymper – and Katherine rushed off to her study to write a poem about him.

It was to be the first of many. After each other, Whym was the love of the Michaels' lives. He arrived at a time of bereavement, just when their house was lacking a male centre. He seemed to possess even more beauty and intelligence than their previous male mentors – and ten times as much as poor Music the Bassett hound, whose ears tended to split. The Michaels wrote poems describing Whym's wolfish, leonine or oriental glamour, his 'ruby head', his 'coat of high strand like mountain juniper', his 'full-furred loveliness'. It particularly gratified Edith and Katherine that whenever they came home Whym leapt from his trance-like state on the rug, greeting them with a 'rage of welcome' and 'what beating of fine, little feet!' They came to see him as a life force, a little sun god, a 'Bacchic cub'.

In the Michaels' passion for Whym Chow, the very English tradition of devotion to pets met fashionable Hindu ideas about the sacredness of animals. 'I suppose our new love of animals is a desire to get into another kingdom,' Katherine wrote perceptively. Whym was not so much a substitute child as a friend who would never let them down, who would love them as mutely and spiritually as their dead, and never say the wrong thing. He also enhanced their passion for each other. Edith called him 'My Love's familiar' (the name for a witch's animal companion) and wrote that she was never really lonely anymore when Katherine was away. 'Watch still beside me,' Katherine wrote to Whym; 'be with me her lover!'

O GOD, NO BLASPHEMY
IT IS TO FEEL WE LOVED IN TRINITY . . .

O SYMBOL OF OUR PERFECT UNION, STRANGE
UNCONSCIOUS BEARER OF LOVE'S INTERCHANGE.

This was a heavy burden of meaning for one small dog to bear. Not surprisingly, it went to his head and he became a tyrant. Whym's reactions to Décor, for instance, had to be respected; 'new furniture had to win his approval.' They quoted him in letters to guests: '*Do* come! Chow says you will, or he will know the reason why.' They never went abroad anymore, and could not bring Whym very far even within Britain; a poem called 'Thou couldst not bear to face the sea' suggests that Whym's panic attacks got in the way of their seaside holidays. All in all, his name begins to sound like a pun on 'whim'.

Ricketts and Shannon had a new publishing house, the Vale Press, which mostly did English classics. They now proved their friendship by making an exception for the plays of the Michael Fields, at a time when no one else would touch them. The first of the Michaels' Roman trilogy, *The World at Auction*, came out in an edition of 210 copies on 24 May 1898. This time there were no quarrels over the illustrations; as well as peacocks, sphinxes and the brooding goddess Fortuna, Ricketts had drawn what they called 'the most beautiful capital letter in the whole world'; the Michaels complained jokily that readers would never get as far as the actual play. Edith had written most of this rather chaotic tragedy about a corrupt second-century Emperor, Didius Julianus, who bribed his way to the top. The most entertaining character is his daughter Clara. Spoilt, arrogant, blunt and bored, she threatens suicide unless her father brings home the crown by dinnertime. 'Everyone I hate / I instantly wish dead', she explains succinctly, and she is not being metaphorical, in a play in which most of the characters have committed at least one murder. The character who most fascinated Edith (she claimed to be 'in love with' him) was Pylades, the beautiful dancer, inspired by Berenson.

For a break, the Michaels went to Yorkshire and the Scottish

Borders, where they attended a bizarre ceremony called the Coronation of the Gypsy King, along with 10,000 Northumberland colliers. They were terrified but also thrilled when the crowd tried to topple the benches the guests were sitting on. In Edinburgh a doctor told Katherine 'she must drink strychnine & arsenic for many months to revivify the nerves'; Edith was more fortunate in only being prescribed salt water rubs.

They came back to reviews of *The World at Auction* by critics who were no longer polite enough to keep the secret of Michael Field's identity, but damned them with faint praise as 'ingenious ladies' and (this was the worst) 'quaint & earnest ladies'. Ricketts wrote with compassionate flippancy to say that Shannon had read that last review aloud over breakfast, causing Ricketts to fall into 'a dead faint'. Katherine wrote to George Meredith to complain that the reviewers were 'all spite-ists'; she hinted heavy-handedly that she would not mind if only a single literary man would speak up in public for the play's virtues – which she then listed. Her tone verged on the paranoid: 'to be left quite alone on Earth with a mob outside execrating, may bring us to the mad house where so many of our friends desire us to be.' Meredith, shocked, wrote back to assure her rather unconvincingly that there was no 'hostility to Michael Field' in the press, it was just that historical drama was out of fashion.

To mark the anniversary of James's death the Michaels went back to Zermatt; after a gruelling soaked day crossing the glacier, Edith fell ill again. In Paris they crossed 'the fiery golden squares as if we were young & had not known grief. A friend invited them to convalesce in Kent, where they walked in the hop gardens, watching the harvest lazily. The night before Katherine's birthday, Edith waited till half past midnight, then laid an exquisite old Berlin ironwork necklace on Katherine's sleeping breast. After all this time, they still treated each other like new lovers.

Their latest tragedy was *Deirdre*, based on an Irish legend. Servant mentors are always important in Michael Field plays, and here there is a fascinating contrast between the nurse Medv, who offers Deirdre simple nurturing, and Lebarcham, the wisewoman and satirist, the bad influence, who encourages the girl's strength of will. Deirdre escapes captivity to run away with the man she loves, but the play's theme is that all you can do is choose one captivity over another: 'Love is the hardest bondage in the world.' This is a moving play in beautifully clear language. Before she kisses her dying husband's bloody wound, Deirdre describes grief as 'One bird's cry on a lake where two have harboured'.

Writing *Deirdre* made them feel unusually sentimental about Ireland in the olden times; they were eager to go there and 'snuff the air' of Celtic romance. But facing the fact that Amy wanted to marry a Dublin doctor, John Ryan, was a different matter. On 28 November Edith recorded 'A letter from Amy, full of ever-kindling love for the little Irish Catholic whose existence we deplore'. Lissie had raised them to think of Catholics as a sinister, priest-ridden people, and the Michaels found John Ryan slow and boring too. But Amy said he was 'warming, waking her'; she seems to have been overjoyed to find someone of her own at last, after a lifetime of playing second fiddle. The Michaels wrote six lines about John Ryan which they scratched out long afterwards – the first of many such retrospective censorings on the same subject. One comment they left legible was 'how horrible is this pressure of the stranger into the privacy of the family'.

However, they were already fantasizing about a life without Amy, without any intruder. December was grim: coal bags dripped black rain across the floor, and all the animals tracked in mud. Katherine and Edith lay in 'our dream-bed' one afternoon and decided it was time to move house. Edith, at thirty-six, felt about eighty. She longed for a break from the past, at last a proper setting for 'the wedded life with my Love in our own home'.

The Forest

He lay asleep, and the long dark season wore:
The forest shadows marked him limb by limb
As on a dial: when the light grew dim,
A steady darkness on the spiny floor,
He lay asleep. The Alpine roses bore
Their last blooms and withered at the rim:
The harvest moon came down and covered him,
And passed, and it was stiller than before.
Then fell the autumn, little falling there
Save some quick-dropping fir-cone on the mound,
Save with the ebbing leaves his own white hair;
And the great stars grew wintry; in the cold
Of a wide-spreading dusk, so woodmen say,
As one asleep on his right arm he lay.

Wild Honey (1908)

1, The Paragon

But where were they to find what Edith called a new 'home for our marriage'? They had only themselves to please; this was to be their final resting-place, their temple of love and beauty.

The year before, the Artists had moved to Richmond, a leafy suburb of London popular with literary and artistic folk, where the two Charleses liked to walk through the parks and study the effects of moonlight. The Michaels now wrote seeking guidance, and possibly an invitation; they hinted that they longed for a river. Fay ordered them to move to Richmond immediately. 'They evidently want us near', wrote Edith, flattered. 'The Artists are more & more our male-doubles'.

For a rent of £70 a year Ricketts and Shannon found the Michaels a narrow Georgian house with a garden that sloped right down to the Thames, and a highly appropriate address: 1, The Paragon. The Painters stood around in the empty house smoking and looking through wallpaper samples, with cries of 'Whew! ... My goodness! ... Creiky!' They showered Katherine and Edith with tiny postcards covered in advice. '*Orange Chrome* is the chrome with the most red in it Painters pretend they cant get it,' Shannon warned them; perfect décor clearly-represented a triumph over the wily working classes.

Meanwhile, unable to get any press to take *Anna Ruina*, Edith and Katherine agreed with the London publisher David Nutt to risk £15 of their own money on it; this was the first time they had to resort to vanity publishing. It appeared in a 'painfully modern' green cover with Russian-looking gold lettering. Though it is one of their best plays, their reputation doomed it, and it got few reviews. A year later it had sold only nineteen copies. 'No wonder I regard publication as merely fire insurance,' commented Edith briskly. At this point they had given up on expanding their audience in England, but an American edition of *Underneath the Bough* (1898) gave them hopes of a new generation of listeners there.

Uprooting themselves from Surrey was not easy. They rented Durdans out, but refused to let the tenants cut down any of the trees. One of the most painful goodbyes was to the gardener who was slowly dying from cancer of the tongue: 'Old George sobbed we were the only friends he had ever known in his life.'

The Painters had the nerve to set off to Italy in April, a month before the move to 1, The Paragon could happen, but they kept sending encouraging postcards. They suggested the Michaels should enter Richmond in a chariot of ivory drawn by leopards. Katherine reminisced in a letter years later:

> *The pards was a detail not carried out; but of Thee, O Bacchus, and of Thy ritual, the open landau piled high with Chow and Field and Michael, doves and manuscripts and sacred plants! – all that is US was there; and we drove consciously to Paradise.*

But Paradise had its rebel angels; Old Sally the cook and Ellen the housemaid, realizing how appallingly steep the stairs were, instantly handed in their notice. Such a betrayal 'brilliantly supported the arguments for slavery', raged Katherine.

Amy stayed with friends and relatives while her engagement dragged on – entirely due, according to the Michaels, to John's cowardice in refusing to marry before he had secured an academic job. They had invited her to be married from Paragon (as they now called their house), adding snidely in their diary that they planned to 'make her as happy as the deplorable marriage-tie she wants a priest to knot can allow us to make her'. They sold many of their best books to pay for a wedding present of an antique silver teapot.

Heterosexuality was disrupting the lives of their 'male-doubles' too. Shannon sometimes had affairs with his female models, and in July, when the Artists came to tea at Paragon, he seemed withdrawn.

> *We think he is in love – or under influence of a woman. There seems that loneliness in Ricketts that comes when 'the fellow' is seduced from devotion to his fellow.*

The four of them had never lived so intimately before; they shopped for furniture by day, took walks by night and watched fireworks on the river. Ricketts was also their most useful critic. 'I beg him to blue-pencil redundant passages that he may help to "unclog" me,' wrote Edith.

In September John Ryan finally found his nerve, and the wedding took place on the 25th. Katherine and Edith did not go to the Catholic ceremony in the local Vineyard Church, but received all the guests afterwards. 'Our quiet little bride', thirty-four and very happy, left by means of a river-boat. Friends wrote with sympathy for their loss of Amy, but all the Michaels felt was '*Rest*'. Now their 'married life' could begin, 'without any impiety', as Edith put it. At Paragon – also known as 'Man Abri' and 'the Doll's House' – they could finally achieve the kind of daily life they wanted, with its rhythms of writing and leisure, privacy and sociability.

The house was one of a row of red- and yellow-brick early nineteenth-century terraces, with five storeys at the back, but only three at the front, and a narrow white Georgian door. 'Do not squirm at the lowly entrance,' they wrote to a friend; 'within the snail-shell are two poets most gay and happy.' The day would begin on the third floor, where the hardworking maids got up long before their mistresses. On the floor below slept Katherine and Edith in their long lacy nightgowns. They had a room each, but they spent every night together, in their curtained bed designed by William Morris, who had died three years before. 'You must have such dreams in that bed,' Ricketts said admiringly. Their rooms were covered in photographs, which included one of the place where James died, one of BB, and seven of Whym. Having spent the night on the couch, Whym would usually wake them by making one clear leap to the bed.

After a long breakfast reading their letters and *The Times* by firelight, Katherine would take the dogs out for their walk along the towpath, striding along like the Archangel Michael, shouting at them when they ran too far. On the first floor was the cool, north-facing Silver Room, where Edith sat and worked under Japanese prints and Shannon's lithographs. The mantelpiece, covered in birds, flowers and fruit, was one of James's carvings; she kept it out of nostalgia, despite Fay's distaste.

From time to time she would take off her little rimless horn glasses and wander through the folding door to see to the exquisite flower arrangements that filled the white-papered Sun Room. Here the eighteenth-century satinwood furniture offered a silken surface for the artfully scattered *objets d'art*: a tangle of jewels on one table top, white porcelain and old glass on another. Every sense was meant to be delighted; one of Ricketts' ideas was to impregnate each drawer of a cabinet with a different scent. The doves cooed in a cage; if they made Edith's head ache she might put them into the tiny glass conservatory attached to the French window to sun themselves. There she could savour the view of Richmond Bridge, its stone arch and row of tall poplars.

The stairs below street level were wainscotted in apple green, like the tiny 'odd-shaped' downstairs Gold Room where they ate their meals. The walls above the panelling were covered in gold Japanese canvas, and there was a small round mirror Ricketts had made them, some glowing Persian plates, and an opal bowl of pot-pourri with an opal shell lying in it. This dining-room led into the tiny 'sulking room' – English for 'boudoir' – which hung over the garden. This cabin, painted green with blue silk cushions and nicknamed the Grot, was where Katherine worked all morning,

Only being a flight of stairs apart, the Michaels could have alerted each other with a call, but they made it a rule not to exchange a word between nine and one. After lunch they poured out the news of what they had written, and made plans for further work, 'breaking bits off for each other to do'. Katherine took most of the responsibility for their contractual affairs and investments, and for writing letters, whether as the public face of Michael Field or as 'dear Mick'. Then there was their diary to write, every few days; what was the point of all this life if it could not be shaped into a narrative?

On many afternoons they gardened, in a spirit of pagan delight. ('I have rubbed myself against Nature's great, warm hand,' Katherine wrote in 1891.) They only regretted that noisy 'loafers & holiday makers' were allowed to use the river tow-path behind their ivy-covered wall. Whym and Musico had a long wire cage to sleep in; the roses had been encouraged to grow over it to mask the mess. There was a shrine to Dionysus in the grass; once they posed Whym asleep at the foot of the altar for a photograph.

In the late afternoon they would generally have a stroll, if Edith's rheumatism allowed it. Ten minutes took them up the road to the Painters' house on Spring Terrace for tea, coffee, or even sloe gin, and talk of jewels, flowers, art and literature. Or the Michaels might have other young men to call, giving them tea in perfect green Italian cups, with shortbread or violet cake. Meanwhile the cook would be down in Paragon's tiny kitchen and old-fashioned smelly scullery, preparing dinner. The Poets would read together, or enjoy a 'long sitting-still' at sunset on their yellow sofa, watching barges pass with their huge headlamps.

The Painters either came to dinner or invited the Michaels almost every Thursday, despite the fact that the Painters' housekeeper Marie, as Katherine recorded, 'does not love us'. These were feasts for the senses. One night, for instance, they had nothing but oysters, which they decided had to be eaten in silence. Katherine and Edith, who used to wear no jewellery but Berlin ironwork, now wore exquisite pendants; Ricketts gave them more than half of all the jewelled art objects he designed.

Formal wear was compulsory at Paragon, which some young guests found rather intimidating. Logan Pearsall Smith described such a dinner many years later, making fun of these 'incredible old maids', who seemed to gradually metamorphose over the course of the evening into chanting priestesses, Maenads, or witches on broomsticks.

Their latest play was a masque, full of magical happenings. At the end of 1899 a small Oxford publisher issued *Noontide Branches* as a thin blue paper pamphlet. Set by a river in the West of England, it has characteristic Michael Field themes such as the ownership of land and the glory of virgins, 'Ye whose spirits have no lord'. Ricketts pointed out that their work was totally humourless, and told them to write a pantomime.

On 21 December, Mary Costelloe's estranged husband died of cancer of the ear, leaving her free to marry BB, which upset both the Michaels. But then, as their friend Amy Bell said cattily, Berenson was only 'a Jewish picture-dealer, not the man for Edith'. Edith repeated this in her diary with snobbish satisfaction.

In the New Year, 'Mary brought a party of the wicked to cigarettes & coffee'. For Edith's thirty-eighth birthday they danced together in the Grot and made Musico drum out 'God Save the Queen' with his paws. Patriotic feeling was running high during the Boer War in South Africa. At Westminster the Home Rulers were demanding some measure of self-government for Ireland, which made Katherine dislike Amy's husband even more. 'Alas, they are a hateful little nest of Catholic pro-Boer Irish mice ... as we have not the same God or the same Country all deep kinship is severed.'

Katherine was suffering from 'nerve-collapse' these days. They were both sick on and off all spring, and after a holiday in the New Forest Edith came down with rheumatic fever and nearly died of a heart attack. 'For days we are severed. She is away in wander-land,' wrote Katherine. She had to lift Edith's limbs to relieve the pain of the swelling, and give her water from a baby's bottle. Amy came to help with the night shifts. In her delirium Edith raved about 'the cocoa-queen' and 'the incorporated bulldogs'.

They enjoyed the convalescence; Edith always felt a great 'spaciousness' after a bad fever. 'My bride, my feast', Katherine called her in a poem. The doctor advised Edith not to attempt the strain of writing for a full year, but poems were flowing from her pen by July. In this mood, even John Ryan's visits were welcome. The Michaels were gradually getting used to his habit of praying during meals, and his appalling puns. He was 'loving & pleased at nonsense', they concluded at last, and 'Amy is happy with him'. At a dinner with the Painters to celebrate the first birthday of the new century, at which they all had two helpings of everything, Edith played a trick on Ricketts by means of an airtube under the cloth, making his plate wobble from side to side. But Ricketts said nothing, assuming it was all due to the champagne.

The mood changed in January 1901 with the news of the death of Queen Victoria and the fall of another cap stone at Stonehenge. They went into mourning: 'Henry is looking like a fresh, black iris.' Dutifully they gummed a picture of the new king Edward VII into their journal, but they were not optimistic about his reign. With such dangerous social tendencies as trade unions, godless science, the extension of the vote and the education of the poor, the twentieth century seemed like a new world of 'lice and scorpions, all things of creeping filth and slime'. About the only modern inventions they welcomed were the electric drill, which reduced Edith's regular agonies in the dentist's chair, and the telephone. Edith was to write in 1905,

> *We have again talked through the telephone – oh, we need nothing but the voice to be to each other. All my Loved is in her generous laugh.*

In 1901 the ten-year nation Census came around, and Edith was amused to find that the form did not accommodate same-sex couples.

Like Shannon, I write myself as head of a house, & like him entertain as guest or lodger the choicest of my sex – the Beloved One, Single & E – even as I am.

Ricketts, who frequently used Edith's face in his woodcuts, was now working on a miniature portrait of her which he intended to put in a pendant called Pegasus and give to Katherine; he got great vicarious pleasure out of their devotion, which seemed more absolute than Shannon's for him.

While the Painters were away in June 1901, a young poet who was 'house-dogging' for them, Thomas Sturge Moore, came to dinner. Tommy or the Albatross, as they nicknamed him, soon came to be one of their dearest friends. 'Tommy is awkward in body as a sturgeon,' commented Edith, 'but he has caviar inside him.' Edith was usually too shy to read her own poems aloud but on one of his six-hour visits Tommy managed to persuade her, and they encouraged him to read his own verse, dramas to them, at least until Whym Chow found the sound disturbing.

Shannon and Rickett's Vale Press now brought out the second play of the Fields' Roman trilogy, *The Race of Leaves*, on gorgeously thick paper with Ricketts' dramatic woodcut decorations, a tide page featuring Janus the two-faced god, black and red lettering, and a green cover with a motif of leaves. The play, mostly by Edith, set at the end of the second century, dramatizes the downfall of the grim Emperor Commodus, whose paranoia begins to seem justified when his sister tries to kill him. His mistress, Marcia, a murderer but also a troubled Christian, is one of the most interesting characters in this play full of bewilderingly complex alliances and rivalries.

In the spring of 1902 there were rats in Paragon. Was nothing sacred? The Michaels escaped to Rottingdean in Sussex for most of April. The worst of it was that the Painters were planning to move away from Richmond; they could not resist a rich patron's offer of spacious penthouse studios in Holland Park. The new place – which the Michaels coldly nicknamed 'The Palace' – was highly aesthetic, even down to its pingpong table, and was crammed with art and antiquities. Ricketts mollified the Poets by telling them that the lift would be strewn with roses whenever they – and Whym Chow – came to dinner.

He also came up with an irresistible subject for a new play: the rise and fall of Sabbatai, the seventeenth-century 'Turkish Messiah'. 'Unless we take the subject quickly,' the Michaels recorded, 'Fay "will give it to [Tommy Sturge] Moore"', his usual threat.' They immediately started sketching out a tragedy about spiritual pride to be called *A Messiah*. Unusually for them, it is only three acts long, and written in a mixture of prose, blank verse and free verse, with choruses who speak in short, bare lines that anticipate the verse dramas of T. S. Eliot. It opens with a chorus of Rabbis watching the man who may be the messiah dip himself in the sea:

THE SEA IS COLD.
THE SEA IS VERY COLD.
THE SEA IS STARRY.
LIKE WOUNDS UPON THE SEA ARE THE LARGE STARS.

Sabbatai is one of their most playful, sensuous heroes; he delights in grapes, coffee, biscuits, and feeds Turkish Delight to children. When captured, his nerve fails and he is forced to convert to Islam. *A Messiah* was a brave stylistic experiment, if not a consistently successful play; the Michaels left it unpublished.

Later in June 1902 Tommy brought along a dinner guest, the Irish poet and playwright William Butler Yeats. Yeats admitted to Edith and Katherine somewhat shyly and in great detail how much he had always admired their plays since his student days. For dinner they all wore wreaths of smilax (climbing asparagus). Edith thought Yeats rather too preachy, however, to be a kindred spirit. She recorded with some amusement how his nervous hands flopped about like flowerheads and his hair 'dribbled' on his forehead; she described how she itched to cut it with the grape-scissors. (They were far from charmed the following year when Yeats asked to see their tragedy *Deirdre* for possible staging by the Abbey, then turned it down, only to produce his own play of the same name in 1907.)

The year before, they had started seeing BB again after a gap of six years. He visited the haven of Paragon quite often these days, but they both found him disappointingly dull as a married man. 'Oh for the days when we discussed sex, & life, & love, & adultery,' sighed Katherine, 'when all things seemed possible – abolition of parents & husbands, duties & ties.'

They spent the summer of 1902 in the New Forest, where Cousin Francis turned up, ever his usual amenable self, even when they tied Whym's leash round his neck and dragged him 'round & round our great mahogany art-table, whisking the whip'. Then they spent October in Rottingdean, where Chow attacked a pet rabbit that belonged to the writer Rudyard Kipling, who lived nearby. They were only slightly sheepish when the rabbit died, and they called Chow 'a young hero'.

The Michaels were spurring themselves on to finish a play about the old Cornish legend of Tristan and Iseult, called *The Tragedy of Pardon*. The heroine's kinswoman Brangaena substitutes herself for her beloved Iseult on the wedding night and submits to Mark's embraces. She even offers to take Iseult's place in a trial by ordeal that involves a branding iron. The Michaels give her an extraordinary speech about the egalitarian and sacred qualities of passion between women.

I CANNOT LET YOU GO. THERE IS LOVE
OF WOMAN UNTO WOMAN, IN ITS FIBRE
STRONGER THAN KNITS A MOTHER TO HER CHILD.
THERE IS NO LACK IN IT, AND NO DEFECT;
IT LOOKS NOR UP NOR DOWN;
BUT LOVES FROM PLENITUDE TO PLENITUDE,
WITH LEVEL EYES, AS IN THE TRINITY
GOD LOOKS ACROSS AND WORSHIPS.

As soon as it was finished they began working on a totally different play about the same story, *Tristan de Léonois*. Yseult (a different spelling to mark the new play) is married to Mark of Cornwall and has already been deserted by her lover Tristan when the tragedy begins. Disguised as a fool, Tristan visits the court; they die by drinking poison together. This play has less suspense and excitement than the first, but what it proves is the richness of the Michaels' imagination; they could create several different visions from the same story.

There was another tragic triangle up the road. On 22 January 1903, Shannon threatened to leave Ricketts and marry his latest model and lover, Hetty Deacon, known as 'Smudge'. Still careful even in his misery, Ricketts recorded the conversation in discreet Italian in his diary and said nothing to the Michaels. He used every possible argument to persuade Shannon to stay: how, for instance, could they possibly divide up their art collection?

Ricketts worked harder than ever; he did yet another editing job on the Michaels' next play, *Julia Domna*, cutting out some of the 'art words' they were so addicted to, before his Vale Press published it in April 1903. Mostly written by Edith, this Oedipal sequel to *The World at Auction* is one of their most powerful and frightening plays. The clarity of its story and theme – two fatherless sons fighting for their mother's love – allows for an exploration of the bonds of blood that goes deeper than cliché. Not only can the widowed Empress Julia not prevent disaster between her sons Caracalla and Geta, but she brings it on, by persuading them to stay with her rather than move apart to a safe distance.

> HOW WILL YOU DIVIDE
> YOUR MOTHER, HOW WILL SHE BE TORN ASUNDER
> AND SHARED BETWEEN YOU?

Caracalla ends up stabbing Geta to death in her arms. But the worst thing for Julia is the realization that she cannot hate Caracalla even now; maternal love is not something holy, but 'a foul canker' in her heart. 'We have no past', Caracalla tells her, with the frightening confidence of a baby; 'Mother and only son as on the day / You gave me birth.'

This riveting play got no critical attention – at this point, critics were simply ignoring anything with 'Michael Field' on the cover – but the beauty of the edition delighted Katherine and Edith. The Vale Press, however, had never recovered from its losses in a big fire two years before; Ricketts had finally to wind it up in June 1903. At least his other misery seemed to be over. Shannon was to keep up a sporadic affair with Hetty Deacon for another four years, but there was no more talk of marriage. That summer Ricketts sent the Michaels some wonderfully camp postcards from the Continent: 'Have no wide notepaper on which to write bluff and manly letter'.

After a visit to Avebury – where Edith was very tempted to burn the village to the ground so that nothing would obscure the standing stones – they went back to Surrey, where the Berensons had established a sort of literary colony at Mary's parents' house in Haslemere. Mary borrowed some pictures from her brother Logan, without asking, to make a nearby cottage beautiful enough for the Michaels to stay there. They walked in the fields talking philosophy with the Harvard professor George Santayana. Berenson teased them by revealing that literary London nicknamed them Gog and Magog (the two legendary giants) and the Scarlet Women. (This last phrase, with its overtones of sexual scandal, probably referred to their plays rather than their love-life, which few would have guessed about.) One day BB finally made Edith a halfhearted apology for his past behaviour: 'I did not suppose you owed me any rancour for the little fracas that happened years ago?' But 'he left me cold,' she wrote. 'I really must do something to hurt Bernhard,' Katherine noted later in the year.

The Michaels had grown to love one of the borrowed pictures in their cottage, a painting on silk. They assumed that Logan had discarded it, and so they took it home with them, as Logan wrote later with tongue-in-cheek tolerance, 'in pious obedience to that law of possession, which, inscribed in Heaven, if not on earth, decrees that objects of beauty belong to those who love them best'. At the time he was less philosophical, and insisted that Mary get it back for him, which caused a breach; the Michaels took years to forgive him for this 'meanness'. They were retreating further and further into eccentricity, a society of two.

In July they had made their wills. Ricketts told them gloomily that to get your papers into the British Library, 'You must be a mummy or George Eliot.' (He would have been very amused to learn that fifty years later, scholars would travel to the British Library's Manuscript Room to pore over the collected Ricketts, Shannon and Michael Field papers.) The Michaels had decided to honour Tommy Sturge Moore by making him their executor, but they were as horrified as Ricketts to hear that Tommy was secretly engaged to his cousin Marie Appia. 'It breaks up that little celebate [sic] company,' Edith wrote, 'and we lose a friend for no man who is married can be a friend.'

But they all rose to the occasion. Ricketts made Marie a stunning jewelled pendant of Psyche descending into Hades, which can be seen as his sly comment on marriage. In 1904, with his usual extraordinary generosity, he designed for Katherine a magnificent mosque-shaped 'Sabbatai ring', inspired by the jewel supposed to have been given to the hero of their play *A Messiah*, to convert him to Islam. These days Ricketts was reading Baudelaire; the Michaels found the 'Femmes Damnées' poems (about passion between women) impressive, though rather over the top. The Painters and Poets discussed how high breasts should be held in a corset.

At Easter, instead of eggs, the Michaels gave each other fine cigarettes and perfume. Early summer saw them in Rottingdean again, walking with Whym and restoring their health with 'good milk puddings'. But what was on their mind was something much spicier. Diane de Poitiers was twenty years older than her lover, Henri II of France; the Michaels represented her as a sexy, white-haired widow, one of their best heroines. Though *Diane: Queen of Earth and Heaven and Hell* centres on the contrast between her and the young, embittered, unloved Queen Catherine de Medici, it is not a cat fight; Diane does try to be a friend to Catherine, though in the best tradition of tragedy it all goes horribly, and mysteriously, wrong.

In a series of letters, Ricketts sent a scenario for a drag tragedy called *Giuliano*, or, *Never, Never Let Us Part*, suggesting they might act it in masks in the Sun Room at Paragon, with Ricketts as Diane (in a mask of silver lace), Katherine as the old King François (pink satin), Edith as Catherine de Medici (black velvet), and Shannon as 'the shut door'. They should exclude all 'inferior married people' from the cast – and, come to think of it, exclude the audience too, since 'art is selfsufficient'.

On a more serious note, though, the Michaels needed a publisher, now the Vale Press had closed. 'God will provide a publisher as he provided a ram for Isaac,' Katherine wrote with grim faith. She asked George Meredith to use his influence in the cause of their five plays which 'must be published', but he could do nothing for her.

In January 1905, Ricketts bullied the politically inert Michaels into getting involved in a protest over the arrest of the Russian writer Maxim Gorky, who was threatened with execution. But Katherine and Edith were more engrossed in another contemporary story of execution. Ras Byzance was an Ethiopian leader who killed his wife and her servants because he suspected her of adultery. The newspaper clipping that alerted the Michaels to the story called it 'A Modern Othello', and indeed, *Ras Byzance*, the stage play Edith wrote in ten days (and it shows), is so feebly reminiscent of *Othello* that a reader would never guess that either the story or writing belonged to the twentieth century.

The Painters wrote from Rome, where Ricketts was giggly with relief; by accident (or perhaps as an unconscious punishment for the 'Smudge' affair?) he had given Shannon eight times the prescribed dose of 'strickneen' for his fever, but Shannon had somehow recovered. In another rather ludicrous health crisis, all the Michaels' doves died of leprosy. Ricketts was very sympathetic, and bought them some more for Easter. But he and Shannon had less patience with those spoilt, barking dogs. Ricketts made frequent jokes about slaughtering them; accepting an invitation to dinner in May, he hinted that 'my lips would relish above all things a Chow ragout in pagoda sauce'.

Back in 1899 he had urged the Michaels to write a play about the Italian Renaissance, with all those 'characters with rich honey & wicked old wine in them'. Once, chatting about the Borgias, Racketts acted out his fantasy of Pope Alexander as an aesthete, fondling a chestful of pearls. This bit of nonsense became a key image in the Michaels' next play, *Borgia*. This steamy, tangled play has a huge cast list of forty-two speaking parts as well as extras, and suffers from a fracturing of the reader's attention and sympathies.

Ricketts was disappointed by this play, but Katherine had learned a crucial lesson from her soured friendship with the Berensons.

> *I don't care a straw what you think of* Borgia *or any other damned play – in comparison with the good of our being 'very pleasant to each other' – like David & Jonathan.*

(What a perfectly homoerotic image for this friendship between a male 'Fairyman' and a female 'Michael'!) Supportive despite his reservations about the play, Ricketts now came up with a great idea. The Michaels should shed their awful reputation by self-publishing *Borgia* anonymously. Ricketts provided the artwork, and sent Tommy Sturge Moore as the intermediary to ask a new publisher – A. H. Bullen – to set his name to it. This simple trick on the critics worked brilliantly. It is ironic that *Borgia*, though one of their worst plays, was the first for many years to get reviews, and a few good ones among them.

After Tommy Sturge Moore, Francis Brooks now had the temerity to get engaged. Though in theory the Michaels could only approve (as they believed 'the unmarried are shelterless & deserted'), they could not help feeling that Katherine had lost her only beau and Edith her best listener. They enjoyed John and Amy's company this summer – he was called 'brother' now, who had once been such an enemy – but the Ryans moved to Dublin in July. The Michaels felt too isolated in September's foul weather to keep a diary.

The Painters were much better at keeping their chins up. When Ricketts's goldfish, Big Ben and Little Billie, both died in October, he sent the Michaels a flippant letter containing a Chinese ode on each fish, with a cartoon of the Dark Angel bearing the two away on a plate. The Poets replied with a Monty-Pythonesque fantasy of 'St Ricketts' restoring the dead to life: 'the fish is not dead, but swooneth'.

Against Ricketts' advice, the Michaels were writing two plays of a planned trilogy about Herod of Israel (persecutor of the Baby Jesus). In their plays he is a moody, schizoid tyrant who puts away his first wife, an Arabian with the unlikely name of Doris, to take a second, Mariamne, whose grandfather he promptly murders. Herod's libido is as nomadic as his conscience, and *Queen Mariamne* is marked by a strong, homoerotic strain in his feelings for his wife's beautiful young brother Aristobulus, whom he watches swimming:

> CARESS ME, O MY DEAR . . .
> O PLUNGED SWAN . . .
>   DIVE DOWN IN THE WATER!
> YOU DAZZLE ME TOO MUCH.

Whereupon, of course, he has the boy drowned. In the second play, *The Accuser*, he has Mariamne put to death, and takes back the powerful white-haired Doris, together with her son Antipater – whose name should surely give his father some hint of danger.

In January 1906 Whym Chow seemed sluggish, which the vet blamed on constipation; 'Whack him, Michael,' advised Ricketts.

This month Katherine met someone who was to prove a crucial new friend: John Gray. His career had paralleled the Michaels', but somehow they had never met. In the 1880s and 90s he had been a dandy and Decadent poet in the Ricketts circle, and a friend and probably lover of Wilde, who took him as the model for the hero of his novel *The Picture of Dorian Gray* (1890) and paid for the printing of Gray's first collection, *Silverpoints* (1893) – praised by one sardonic critic for the beauty of its margins. Just two years later Gray began to change his life by buying up copies of *Silverpoints* and destroying them. He formed a lifelong partnership with the

Michaels' old acquaintance Marc-André Raffalovich, who had argued in *Uranisme et Unisexualité* (1896) that homosexuals were born, not made, but should sublimate their feelings into friendship. In 1898 Gray became a priest, which Ricketts told all round town as a runny story. Ricketts finally introduced Katherine to the 'rosy', golf-playing Canon Gray at the Palace on 26 January 1906.

She went home that night and found Whym Chow walking into walls. Eight years old, he was suddenly blind and in great pain, evidently 'stricken of some awful brain disease'. She and Edith nursed him round the clock, and wrote to Ricketts of their terror. Two days later, they decided to have Whym put down. Katherine wanted it to be done with one clean bullet, but guns were forbidden in Richmond; after six hours of bungled efforts with sleeping draughts, he died. By terrible luck, it was just then that they received Ricketts' answer to their last letter; he told them he was sick of their 'morbid preoccupation' with the petty illnesses of their spoiled pet. 'Well may he be jealous,' Edith raged; 'Michael & I love Chow as we have loved no human being.'

On 1 February they buried Whym Chow under the altar of Dionysus in the garden, with an eclectic service that included one of John Gray's Catholic poems; Katherine wore a black hat with horse plumes. They went to Rottingdean for a break, but every walk, retraced in floods of tears, reminded them of the dog. Parodic odes were all very well for Ricketts' goldfish, but for Whym Chow they began writing an entire book of poems, published years later in a terracotta suede limited edition under the unabashed title, *Whym Chow: Flame of Love*. Any reader expecting sentimental Victorian pet poems will be unnerved by this collection, in which Whym features as sex symbol and god made flesh, the masculine principle joined with their womanhood in a mystic trinity. Just as they had reinterpreted James Cooper as soon as they lost him, so the Michaels rewrote the death of this 'doomed little wanderer' as a Christ-like sacrifice. They claimed that the intensity of his love had caused his fife to be 'consumed' after only eight years, and that he was now their 'guardian angel' or spirit guide.

Condolence letters poured in. Logan Pearsall Smith recalled thirty years later how his sister Mary Berenson sat up till four in the morning trying to write an adequately sad letter, but her brisk advice on good places abroad where they might cheer up seemed 'barbaric' to Edith. She and Katherine were having a sort of joint breakdown. Months later Ricketts complained that the Michaels' letters were still 'stilted & lacrymose'. He was going through a dreadful time himself, because Shannon was in love with a model again – the twenty-six-year-old free-spirited sculptor Kathleen Bruce, who was looking for the ideal man to father the son she longed for. 'What should I do if Shannon got married?' Ricketts wrote in his diary later that year. The Michaels had no idea about this anxiety which preyed on his nerves. His letter to them of 9 April is a strange mixture of the irritated ('I won't listen to any more laments') and the whimsical ('slay the fatted muffin in anticipation of my return'). They responded with rage to what Edith called his 'sulphurous & vile jeering', and for two months it looked like this friendship, central to all their lives, might fall apart. Then at the end of June, Katherine and Edith paid a visit to Shannon and Ricketts, all being very careful with each other.

In August they made the first of their trips to see the Ryans in Dublin. They came home via Scotland, so Edith could be introduced to John Gray and Marc-André Raffalovich in Edinburgh. Canon Gray, whose past had overlapped with the Michaels', could understand their hunger for something more, now Whym Chow was dead, some consolation no human friend could give. With his discreetly homoerotic side, he was the perfect bridge between two pagan lesbians and an institution they had been raised to loathe: the Roman Catholic Church.

In retrospect, their conversion seems inevitable. As Katherine and Edith saw it, Whym Chow's divine sacrifice of his life had made them understand that of Jesus, and won them salvation. To put it another way, it could be said that the Michaels were so lonely and isolated after their dog's death that they needed a new kind of ready-made family. But why should such free spirits have picked one of the most authoritarian and repressive churches around?

Dionysiac ritual was not enough for them; it had no real structure, offered no company, and could not tell them how to live their lives. Though Katherine had attended the Anglican Church sporadically over the years, it had always seemed to both of them rather wishy-washy and hollow, an altar with nothing on it. Whereas the Roman Catholic Church appealed to their sense of drama and sacred ritual, as well as offering a clear, disciplined and sociable path to heaven. It was ancient and regal; its décor, all gold and incense, could have come straight out of one of their plays. It promised a God they could literally bow down to and take into their mouths, as well as real communion with the dead; it demanded absolute surrender in return.

Such a conversion was also highly fashionable. Victorian women writers and 'inverts' of both sexes, in particular, were turning Catholic in their droves. Literary lesbians who made the crossing in the early twentieth century included Radclyffe Hall and Una Troubridge, Renée Vivien and Violet Shiletto, 'Tony' Atwood and 'Christopher' St John, and Alice B. Toklas. Being Catholic in England meant becoming slightly foreign, aloof from the establishment; as a church it was associated with the rich and the poor, but definitely not the bourgeoisie. And although Catholic women were meant to be subordinate to men, they could also devote themselves to the barely veiled goddess-cult of the Virgin Mary. 'O virgin life, O vowed and deep secluded / O angel-sung!' wrote the Michaels a few years later. Suddenly being spinsters was something holy.

Their journals, from the winter of 1906 on, are a sort of spiritual travel diary. Edith decided to move her birthday from 12 January to 29 October (Whym Chow's birthday), to mark the dog's role as 'God's Minister' in her life. By December 1906 they were going to Mass regularly, reading a Latin Missal (early nineteenth-century Venetian, of course) and recording their amazement that the year of their 'worst loss' was also the time of their greatest 'marvel'.

Although converting to Catholicism was yet another way for the Michaels to remain united, each needed to make the journey on her own. Katherine's confessor (a priest who would advise her as well as hearing her Confession) was Father Vincent McNabb, an Irish Dominican. Edith hated him on sight for his 'supercilious hardness', but within a month he had become 'the great Vincent', a dear figure in his big black cloak. McNabb was an easygoing man who used to annoy them by giggling in church; he assured Katherine that 'the Church welcomes poets' and supported the Michaels as a couple, writing after their deaths of their unique 'fellowship in life and love'. Edith's confessor at the local Vineyard Church in Richmond was a young curate from Amiens in Northern France, Father Gosscannon, which she soon shortened to 'Goss' or 'Gossie'. A skinny, livery, moody man with beautiful marble hands, whose vestments were always too short, he 'broke me in and trained me', she reported. Had they met 'in the world', she admitted years later, there would have been 'attraction' between them. The confession box provided a safe setting for the kind of intense, flirtatious friendship both the Michaels liked to have with men; the Church had solved the problem of friendship between the sexes, Edith wrote playfully, because 'the Priest is Man on Woman's terms'. There was 'no love lost' between McNabb and Goss, which the Michaels found quite amusing. And for extra advice and consolation they both had John Gray, whom Katherine nicknamed 'Father Silverpoints' so he would never forget their shared past. John Ryan was an influence not only on them but on his wife; Amy, in Dublin, made the decision to convert at exactly the same time, Easter 1907.

But the Michaels still had last-minute worries. They knew they would have to surrender many things, in particular the freedom to decide on the rightness of things for themselves. As usual, Edith was the only one who dared write down anything about their sex life. She referred to 'my secret sins' obliquely on 9 April: how could she speak to Father Goss of the anguish of the 3rd, 4th & 5th Verses of *Femmes Damnées*?' Baudelaire's two 1857 poems of that name were banned in France till 1947. In the verses in question in the longer of the poems, the nervous younger woman, Hippolyte, is described as weeping, whereas her seducer, Delphine, is shown '*étendue à ses pieds, calme et pleine de joie*' ('stretched at her feet, calm and satisfied'). By the time we reach verse thirteen, Hippolyte has mustered enough strength to ask whether they have committed '*une action étrange*' ('a peculiar act'), but Delphine soothes her conscience, and the women end the poem in an eternal, though damned, embrace.

This might seem like a strange allusion for Edith, whose sense of her bond with Katherine had always seemed so joyful, but now she was entering a Church which said that all sex outside marriage was sinful. The problem was whether Goss was educated enough to pick up the reference to Baudelaire, or would she have to spell it out? 'And I know he thinks I have to confess forbidden relations to men,' she wrote in exasperation, 'with whom the relations of my lifetime have been abstract & blameless.'

On 12 April Edith panicked and sent Katherine running off to tell Goss to cancel the baptism scheduled for the 19th. 'There is nothing this young seminarist might not misconceive ... even our Sacred Relation to each other!' Confused, but kind, Goss persuaded her to calm down. Before her first Confession, Edith prayed 'that the Christ so exquisite to women may inform my young Confessor'. In fact it was a very soothing, general Confession. Edith made a 'vow of chastity' as a gift to God at this time, and Goss did not probe. Katherine made her own first Confession and, as Edith recorded with a little defiance, *comes straight down the Church to me, bearing a kiss ready on her lips . . . while the Priest prays she presses the kiss home with a brave sound . . . The Priest heard.*

In those days, priests seem to have had no objection to such loving converts, or such audible kisses.

Edith was baptized by Goss at the Vineyard Church in Richmond on 19 April 1907. Amy, in Dublin, followed suit on 1 May. Katherine waited till Gray could receive her on 8 May (the feast of St Michael) at his new church in Edinburgh. Only then did she write to Ricketts.

Being a serpent & so wise I trust this news will not startle you; for you must have seen how 'the ruddy Mass Book' has been with us all the winter . . .' I invoke your Catholic mother of the many lovely names to plead with you to be glad.

Ricketts was shocked, but sent gallant congratulations; he would only resent their conversion, he wrote, if he found his seat in Paragon usurped by the '*chers pères*' ('dear fathers', i.e. priests). Despite being an atheist, he threw himself into helping his friends accessorize; he gave them his mother's coral rosary, portable candlesticks, a crucifix and a small Spanish reliquary with fragments of the True Cross. On one of his later visits Edith absentmindedly called him 'Father', which he found hilarious. Ricketts was feeling very relieved in 1907, as Kathleen Bruce had decided against marrying Shannon, having met a much more impressive father for her unborn children: Captain Robert Scott. (She had the son she always wanted, and shared her husband's adventurous life for a couple of years before he died in a tent near the South Pole in March 1912.)

In one sense, the Michaels' conversion can be seen as a disaster. Instead of spending their days thinking about art and love, they now fretted over the finer points of Catholic theology, such as whether Edith might be allowed to bend the rules of fasting because of her difficulty digesting fish. But on the other hand, 'Sancta' or 'Holy Mother Church' was like a new lover to Katherine and Edith: 'our whole lives are filled with happiness because of her', they insisted. Just after her baptism, Katherine wrote Edith this short poem.

BELOVED, NOW I LOVE GOD FIRST
THERE IS FOR THEE SUCH SUMMER BURST
WHERE IT WAS STIRRING SPRING BEFORE,
LO, FOR THY FEET A BLOSSOM-FLOOR!

PATIENCE! A LITTLE WHILE TO WAIT
TILL I POSSESS MY NEW ESTATE,
THEN TO ASSUME THY GLORIOUS PART
IN MY ENRICHED AND FEASTING HEART.

It took patience, and flexibilty, but their love did weather this great change. Like many long-term couples who do not have sex anymore, the Michaels remained extraordinarily intimate. They still had breakfasts in bed 'for revel', and romantic holidays. On 7 December 1907 in Confession, Edith had to admit to 'shameless dallyings with most perilous temptation, all the more base & ungrateful as, since I entered the Holy Catholic Church, I have never fallen into fleshly sin'. Goss took this calmly and advised her to focus on the purity of the Virgin Mary.

Another likeable thing about their conversion was that they did not write off their past as one long sojourn in the wilderness. There was some breast-beating over their Decadent days, but mostly they saw their pagan worship as having been a helpful preparation for the real thing. They kept on writing, though literature was no longer quite at the centre of their lives. Edith claimed that it helped her poetry to have a meaningful focus, rather like being in love. Their 1908 collection, *Wild Honey from Various Thyme*, mixed poems from the 1890s (on nature, classical themes and love) with new religious ones. Despite his protestation that he could not draw bees, Ricketts designed them a honeycomb cover for this book which contains some of their best work, especially Katherine's sequence of sonnets on James's death in the forest. Another very moving poem begins:

LORD LOVE. TO THY GREAT ALTAR I RETIRE;
TIME DOTH PURSUE ME, AGE IS ON MY BROW,
AND THERE ARE CRIES AND SHADOWS OF THE NIGHT.
TRANSFORM ME, FOR I CANNOT QUIT THEE NOW.

In many ways life went on as normal after the Michaels' conversion. They were more cheerful – except when they wept during Confession – and less isolated. They went to Dublin yearly, and in 1908 they visited the Berensons in Italy, where Mary made them a portfolio of Italian religious paintings – 'In this way even a heathen may be helpful!', she commented ruefully. Their old acquaintance Will Rothenstein came back into their lives in 1906, and the Michaels grew very close to 'Billy' and his wife and child.

They went on many retreats to convents – despite their dislike of nuns – and Katherine visited workhouses, where she caused one deathbed conversion which gave Edith a pang of 'spiritual envy'. But they also still enjoyed choosing hats, and good food. Even when in 1910 they became Dominican tertiaries (like lay nuns), they got a special dispensation to keep going to the theatre. They also remained interested in current affairs, such as the dreadful 1906 scheme to build a 'Channel Tunnel' between Britain and France. (They need not have worried so prematurely, as the 'Chunnel' did not open till 1994.)

In January 1909 they received a feverish scrawl from Amy – still 'our Little One' in her mid-forties. Pneumonia, in those days, had no treatment but aspirin and morphine. Katherine and Edith made the gruelling journey to Dublin by train and boat; as the Ryans' house was full, they stayed at a hotel, where they were bewildered by the strangeness of electric light in their bedroom. 'The nurse-fiend' insisted that the shock of their arrival would harm Amy, so for several days they had to creep about the house, rearranging the withered flowers, whispering to 'Johnnie'. When they finally insisted on going in, Amy was overjoyed to see them, but her breath sounded 'like flight on flight of warlike arrows', wrote Edith, making an Amazon of her dying sister. Again, the nurse tried to make them leave husband and wife alone together, but John had already arranged the deathbed: Katherine was to hold Amy's hand, and Edith was to sit directly in her line of vision to the last.

His generosity lasted past Amy's death. 'John wants to bring her back to us,' wrote Edith. Crowds of the poor Amy had helped filed in to pay their respects, and then 'the new trio' set off for the boat to England with Amy's body shrouded in a nun's habit. They buried her in Mortlake cemetery in Richmond. Edith was briefly racked with guilt for neglecting her sister all her life, and distressing her with her 'modernism'; she cried so much that she went blind for a while in February. But even when Musico the Bassethound died later in the spring, their losses did not shatter the Michaels as they would have in the pre-conversion days. The Church provided a structure both for grief and the hope of meeting again, and Katherine had an unorthodox faith that 'of course there are dogs in our Father's House – & pleasant baying sounds'.

These days they had enough spirit and humour to weather health crises and the financial horrors caused by Edith's income being tied up in probate with her sister's (and also John wanting to break Amy's will in order to give more to charity). They sent a self-mocking invitation to the Rothensteins:

> *'We are gradually gathering together the teeth, glasses, wigs, and complexions that may enable us again to greet our friends.'*

Just as they held onto their non-Catholic friends, so they were still proud of their pre-Catholic writings. They were sometimes a little embarrassed by them, but made no attempt at self-censorship;

in fact, with McNabb's encouragement they got around to publishing several more plays from the bottom drawer. As he assured them, 'it is by truthful expression of the whole of our lives that the value of our conversion is assured'; theirs was a story with a holy ending. Using the persona of 'the author of *Borgia*', a nameless, reclusive male, they published *Queen Mariamne* in 1908, and arranged to bring out five more *(The Tragedy of Pardon, Diane, The Accuser, Tristan de Léonois and A Messiah)* in 1911. A clever preface claimed that 'the author of *Borgia*' had died in Rome after years of illness and was buried in an unmarked grave, but hinted that further 'hidden manuscripts' of his might yet 'be found, like a squirrel's hoard'. Probably they planned to publish their four remaining pre-Catholic plays, but then to turn to the great work of writing plays for God. Now, as they saw it, their new career could begin.

Mortal, if thou art beloved'

Mortal, if thou art beloved
Life's offences are removed:
All the fateful things that checked thee
Hearten, hallow and protect thee.
Grow'st thou mellow? What is age?
Tinct on life's illumined page,
Where the purple letters glow
Deeper, painted long ago.
What is sorrow? Comfort's prime,
Love's choice Indian summer-clime.
Sickness? Thou wilt pray it worse
For so blessed, balmy nurse.
And for death? When thou art dying
Twill be love beside thee lying.
Death is lonesome? Oh, how brave
Shows the foot-frequented grave!
Heaven itself is but the casket
For love's treasure, ere he ask it,
Ere with burning heart he follow,
Piercing through corruption's hollow.
If thou art beloved, oh then
Fear no grief of mortal men!

Underneath the Bough (1893)

We can never part

'The year will not be dull,' wrote Edith confidently, looking forward to 1911. In fact, it was to bring the crowning drama of her life – finally, a tragedy worthy of her talents. In late January, just after her forty-ninth birthday, she was diagnosed with terminal cancer.

She and Katherine decided to get a new dog without delay. Edith found her bed painful, so 'We get pillows & down-quilt – in each other's arms we sleep on the floor, cherishingly.' After the initial shock there was a time of coming to terms; as they expressed it in typically colourful fashion in a letter to the Rothensteins, 'We had to go into Arabian deserts to repossess our souls.' Removing the tumour was impossible; all that was available was 'a hideous operation of alleviation'. Edith refused it, and tried treating herself with a decoction of violet leaves in Lourdes water – a suitable mixture of the floral and the mystical.

The Michaels turned to their priests and got immense support. Whatever the effect of conversion on their writings, it provided a storyline that made sense of pain. Her cancer was a penance, Edith wrote, for her 'great, flagrant sinning' of the past – but also an opportunity for her to develop courage and peace in following Jesus to Calvary. She was convinced, too, that her spiritual progress was helping Amy to graduate from Purgatory to Heaven.

Her illness renewed many of her friendships, even with those who had been cast out of the circle, such as Logan Pearsall Smith. Ricketts visited frequently, with plants, rose-leaf conserves, or very good chocolate. 'I never thought the freakish aesthete of the Vale could be so brotherly in sweetness of charity to those stricken by sorrow & disease,' wrote Edith. The Berensons sent a Chinese carpet, which made Ricketts jealous; Katherine wrote to reassure him that moths were devouring it. 'How much I have loved you,' wrote Berenson to Edith; he was shocked into this uncharacteristic declaration. On one visit he held her foot in its slim French shoe as if unwilling to let her go.

A new dog arrived on approval – a sagging, bandy-legged Elkhound, suffering from canker and worms. Edith could not resist him and cancelled the order to send him back; they named him Ferrar or the Elk. Katherine was amazed by Edith's heightened zest for life:

TO SEE HOW ALL THE WORLD IS GROWING NEW
TO THEE, O LOVED, NOW THOU ART DOOMED TO DIE!

'When the pain is very bad,' Edith wrote at Easter 1911, 'Michael takes me in her arms, & the vital warmth of her being is of such power the pain goes to sleep.' Edith had the odd glass of cognac, but consistently refused the morphine that had helped her mother and grandmother in their dying. This was so that she could carry on writing, and keep her wits about her, but also to maintain a strong will throughout the spiritual struggle, and suffer some part of what Jesus did. She gripped her crucifix as a sort of lightning rod to let the pain pass right through her. For Katherine, having to watch this was nearly as hard. 'I am all dirty from the battle, and smoked, and bleeding,' she wrote to a friend; '– often three parts dragon myself to one of Michael – and sometimes I have only clenched teeth to offer to God.' But neither of them did lose faith.

A powerful new drug, Trypsin, meant that Edith's 'exercise in dying', as she called it, took nearly three years. It was a mixed blessing, but she was grateful for every extra day. She wrote as fast as she could but also enjoyed travelling in a rather unreliable new motor car. At the end of 1911 'Master & Little Laddie' faced into another year with 'a vast exhilaration', according to Edith; at midnight they put on their Dominican scapulars (cloaks) and sang a 'marriage-song'. In early 1912 they made a further Solemn Profession as a sort of joint marriage to Jesus: 'the two gold rings & the lovely spousals ... Brides of the Heavenly Bridegroom together'. In March Katherine fell downstairs and broke her right wrist, which disrupted their usual roles; suddenly Edith had to do the packing. Both needing not to be jolted, they had to sleep in separate rooms for the first time ever, which distressed them.

Their first religious poems had been a little twee, but the horrors of sickness and imminent death gave their new work a sense of passionate urgency. In April 1912 they published *Poems of Adoration*, almost entirely by Edith. These poems characterize Christ as a virile and demanding lover, whether he is sacrificing himself or demanding sacrifice.

> THY OWN BODY THOU DIDST TAKE
> IN THY HOLY HANDS – AND BREAK.

Religious poetry can suffer from a sort of smug flatness, as if there is an answer to every question. But this collection is impressive at times. In 'Unsurpassed', Edith uses a wonderful image of death as escape from the body.

> OH, LET ME RUN TO THEE, AS RUNS A WIND
> THAT LEAVES THE WITHERED TREES, IT MOVED, BEHIND,
> AND TRIUMPHS FORWARD, CARELESS OF ITS WAKE!

She was also working at top speed on what would be their last play, *Iphigenia in Arsacia*, an interesting three-acter about St Matthew and a girl he raises from the dead. Iphigenia feels full of new life, yet also melancholy; having vowed her virginity to God in impulsive gratitude for her resurrection, she now has to give up her lover and become a nun. It is a play about solemn vows, about keeping your word even if it kills you; it ends with the nun and saint getting martyred together.

Being so preoccupied with her work and her dying, Edith sometimes forgot to pay attention to Katherine, who could feel 'severed' from her. Coming back from a holiday, Edith could not walk up the stairs of Paragon, and asked for the sturdy maid Josephine to support her; miserably jealous, Katherine sat in the car and tore out a bit of her own silvery hair. 'You must nurse your nurse.' McNabb reminded Edith. She began spending the capital she would not need much longer; she adapted Paragon to suit invalids (piping hot water upstairs to spare the maids' legs) and lavished 'love gifts' on Katherine. She had new blue and white silk curtains hung in the Sun Room where she now lived day and night on the couch, propped up on silk cushions, swathed in quilts and black lace wraps, with a little table of flowers to hand. On New Year's Eve 1912, she sat up for two and a half hours, scribbling – in her now almost illegible handwriting – a twenty-page summary of the year. Her energy came from knowing that any day might be her last.

'Poor Field is off and on about her dying,' Mary Berenson wrote in exasperation to a friend; 'Michael is such an idiot as to refuse to have a nurse to help her, even with the surgical part.' Loyal, for all her bitchiness, Mary offered to rent the Michaels a little house in Hampstead, as Paragon was more and more impracticable. Katherine accepted promptly and asked Mary to come home from Italy and help them move, but Mary wrote to a friend that she simply could not spare the time, though she knew they would think her a 'traitor'.

At one point, dropsy – the illness Edith hated most – meant that her legs had to be punctured to drain them, and her throat produced 'a sound like that of a dove that fights against choking corn'. Katherine turned this squalid symptom into an extraordinary poem.

SHE IS SINGING TO THEE, DOMINE!

DOST HEAR HER NOW?
SHE IS SINGING TO THEE FROM A BURNING THROAT,
AND MELANCHOLY AS THE OWL'S LOVE-NOTE;
SHE IS SINGING TO THEE FROM THE UTMOST BOUGH
    OF THE TREE OF GOLGOTHA, WHERE IT IS BARE,
AND THE FRUIT TORN FROM IT THAT FRUITED THERE;
SHE IS SINGING . . . CANST THOU STOP THE STRAIN,
    THE HOMAGE OF SUCH PAIN?
DOMINE, STOOP DOWN TO HER AGAIN!

Katherine was not proud of the poems in her last book, *Mystic Trees*, by comparison with Edith's *Poems of Adoration*; she thought they addressed God with too much familiarity and not enough awe. But that is exactly what makes hers more moving to a modern reader. There are many simple, intimate poems to Jesus and to Mary, who in one poem is described as the 'apple on the topmost bough' – an image from Sappho. But the most interesting are Katherine's poems about Edith's death. They can be read in the tradition of the late Victorian obsession with the beautiful dying woman, but they stand out because of their urgently autobiographical tone and emphasis on unglamorous pain. In these unresolved, despairing poems Katherine is storming Heaven.

OH. WHAT CAN DEATH HAVE TO DO
WITH A CURVE THAT IS DRAWN SO FINE,
WITH A CURVE THAT IS DRAWN AS TRUE
AS THE MOUNTAIN'S CRESCENT LINE? . . .
LET ME BE HID WHERE THE DUST FALLS FINE!

One poem called 'Lovers', Katherine left unpublished; it describes them as literally knotted together.

LOVERS, FRESH PLIGHTING LOVERS IN OUR AGE
LOVERS IN CHRIST – SO TENDER AT THE HEART
THE PULL ABOUT THE STRINGS AS THEY ENGAGE –
ONE THING IS PLAIN: – THAT WE CAN NEVER PART.

When Katherine wrote this she could have had no idea how true it would turn out to be. In June 1913, at the age of sixty-six, she was diagnosed with breast cancer. This could be attributed to heredity, age, the stress of nursing Edith – or a determination not to be left behind. She was offered an operation that might have saved her life or at least lengthened it, but she refused.

The Michaels had shared every tiny detail of their lives, but now, with a wonderful irony, just when Katherine needed Edith's sympathy most, she was too generous to cause her pain by telling her. She never breathed a word of her secret in their diary; apart from her doctor, only Gray and McNabb knew. As far as Edith was aware, Katherine simply had some heart trouble, which Edith thought the doctor was exaggerating.

Staying in Hampstead that summer, they were neighbours to Tommy and Maria Sturge Moore; the four became very close. Katherine read Wordsworth to Edith, just as she had to her dying sister and mother. In the intervals between her bad times, Edith made notes on what agony was teaching her:

> It is a great solitude. And I have been able to think of things with a quietness I would not have lost. . . . Pain is so real it may even be a key to the fresh motions of childhood. It makes all things new.

Back in Paragon, 'faithful Francis' visited, and Edith, most unusually, decided to read her cousin Katherine's love poems to herself from the last quarter-century; 'I believe it is only to him I could read what is so thrilling and sacred to my heart.' Now Katherine could hear what 'her poet-lover's gift' had meant to Edith. 'It is infinitely soft between us,' wrote Katherine. 'Warm buds open.'

On 25 November Edith stopped writing her diary and saved all her energy for prayer. Ricketts visited with clay angels and a camel laden with pearls for her Crib. She and Katherine had planned her deathbed with McNabb nearly two years before. Katherine had been afraid that she would feel distanced, cut off from her Beloved by the formality of the sacraments and prayers. 'Oh, but you will be Master,' McNabb had assured her. Edith's last words showed her endless appetite for life: 'Not yet, not yet.' She died on 13 December 1913.

Katherine's main emotion was relief 'Now she is her crisp, delicious, gay and gamesome Ariel spirit of old.' Edith was buried at Isleworth, near Richmond, with a few friends attending. The funeral brought on Katherine's first haemorrhage. 'Two days after thou wert gone, bleeding came,' Katherine told Edith in her diary, relieved to be honest with her at last. A nun came to nurse Katherine and dress the abcess in her breast – 'She is not a pretty little nun, Hennie,' Katherine reassured her dead lover coyly. (By February, the nun had got over-attached, and was kissing Katherine all the time and complaining sadly that she knew 'she could not be like the companion'.)

Knowing she would not have long to wait, Katherine lived through the next nine months fairly peacefully, 'quiet as a plough laid by at the furrow's end', as one poem described old age. Another poem, 'I am thy charge, thy care!', captured her sense that Edith was still hovering round her, praying for death to join them. Katherine was coming to realize that their conversion to Catholicism, however good it had been for their souls, had sometimes distracted them from each other. 'Show me how you love me now.' she wrote to Edith.

Katherine's natural vitality kept her working: she brought out a limited edition of twenty-seven copies of *Whym Chow: Flame of Love* for their friends, and collected Edith's early poetry in a volume called *Dedicated*, published by 'Michael Field' as usual, with yet another beautiful cover by Ricketts. She even had enough energy for quarrels. The Berensons, who disliked her executor Tommy

Sturge Moore, told her that she had no right to bequeath to him her diaries which were full of the Berensons' uncensored conversations. (To think, Mary wrote to a friend, that they had once considered the Michaels 'real friends instead of literary monsters'!) Katherine also had a ridiculous battle with Ricketts. On and off all spring, she kept nagging him to pay a memorial visit to the Sun Room where Edith had spent so many months before she died, until he finally walked out of the house, 'I believe to save himself from striking me'. But she knew that she and Ricketts loved each other too much to sulk for long, and a fortnight later she made her will, with him and Shannon as the chief beneficiaries.

By the summer of 1914 Katherine was weakening; she stopped writing, and moved to a cottage near Hawksyard Priory in Staffordshire, to be near Father McNabb. (She knew, as she shut the door of 1, The Paragon, that she would never be back.) Like Oscar Wilde, she was troubled by the décor: 'I am suddenly asked to die in a stuffy drawing room with a grand piano, & lusters & every form of vulgar & horrible details.' But outside her window was an overgrown lawn, at least, so she made the best of things and named the place 'Paragon Cottage'.

World War One broke out on 5 August, ending the world Katherine had known. Jenny the cook burst in to say, 'Good news; fifty thousand Germans killed!' Katherine was appalled by this bloodthirstiness, but also oddly excited. All in all this was a happy period; the nurse reported that Katherine smiled all night in her sleep. On 18 September the chaotic handwriting in the diary finally came to a halt. But Katherine continued to get up every day at seven and have herself wheeled into the Priory in a Bath chair to hear Mass. On 26 September 1914 she wrote to Ricketts first thing in the morning. The nurse was dressing her for Mass when Katherine fell into her arms and died.

The mummy invokes his soul

Down to me quickly, down! I am such dust,
Baked, pressed together; let my flesh be fanned
With thy fresh breath; come from thy reedy land
Voiceful with birds; divert me, for I lust
To break, to crumble – prick with pores this crust! –
And fall apart, delicious, loosening sand.
Oh, joy, I feel thy breath, I feel thy hand
That searches for my heart, and trembles just
Where once it beat. How light thy touch, thy frame!
Surely thou perchest on the summer trees ...
And the garden that we loved? Soul, take thine ease,
I am content, so thou enjoy the same
Sweet terraces and founts, content, for thee,
To burn in this immense torpidity.

Wild Honey (1908)

Epilogue

The largest legacy Katherine left was £2000 to Ricketts and Shannon; it was much depleted by the war by the time they received it, but it did pay for a pianola to keep their spirits up. She left a mass of poetry in manuscript to a Catholic friend, Emily Fortey, but the bulk of the Michael Field papers were left to Tommy Sturge Moore: twenty-eight white vellum volumes of their journals, as well as several volumes of miscellanea. The will gave dauntingly specific instructions: he was to leave *Works and Days* unopened for fifteen years ('we do not want it to do harm' to the living, they had written when drafting their will), and then publish a book of selections plus letters forming 'a connected biography'. Fifteen years was not long; they were clearly impatient to become posthumously famous.

The Michaels considered that they were honouring 'dear Tommy' with this legacy, especially considering their reservations about him as a non-Catholic. But they could not have chosen better. For the rest of his life, Sturge Moore preserved, annotated and published selections from the Michael Field papers, promoting them in every way.

As for the Artists, Shannon had his first major solo exhibition in 1929; when he was rehanging a picture at home after it, he fell off a ladder onto the marble flagstones and suffered terrible brain damage. Ricketts sold many of their treasures to pay for nurses. He flung himself into work and travel; after two years, his own health failed and he died in 1931, but Shannon lived on till 1937.

As executor they too had chosen Tommy Sturge Moore, and he worked just as hard to promote their memory.

When at the end of 1929 he had opened Katherine and Edith's diaries, as instructed, it must have taken him months on end to read them, even with his son's help in deciphering the handwriting. Quite apart from the passages of erotic devotion, the Michaels had left so many indiscreet or malicious remarks about people who were still alive that he could not possibly have put together selections amounting to a full life. The single volume of *Works and Days* published in 1933, after another five years' hard work, focused on the Michaels' literary friendships.

Writing lesbian history often depends almost entirely on the integrity of executors. To his great credit, Sturge Moore destroyed nothing, and left the Michael Field papers neatly indexed in the British Library for a less shockable generation. And a century after their small peak of fame in the 1890s, the Michael Fields are beginning to be rediscovered by critics and readers. As the speaker urges in a 1908 poem called 'A Palimpsest',

LET US WRITE IT OVER,
O MY LOVER,
FOR THE FAR TIME TO DISCOVER.

Their work is very hard to get hold of. *Underneath the Bough* (reprinted in 1993 with *Sight and Song*) and *Long Ago* are probably their best poetry collections. The plays are harder to read, but long overdue for reassessment. Some of the plays most deserving of new readers are not the best known: I would particularly recommend *Anna Ruina*, *Stephania*, *The Cup of Water*, and *Julia Domna* (which might work especially well on stage).

In 1923 Ricketts was shocked to hear that their graves – Katherine's at Hawksmoore Priory, Edith's at Isleworth – were unmarked. Despite his fading eyes he designed a black marble slab with white moulding, 'the Michael monument' as he called it, and got John Gray to think of an inscription: 'United in blood, united in Christ'. But everything that could go wrong with the monument did. No sooner was it erected, in November 1926, than it cracked loudly, frightening the local priest, and the pieces had to be dragged away and bolted back together.

Books, luckily, are the headstones that never fall.

A few months after Edith's death, John Gray tried to explain to Katherine that the Church could not say for sure whether her dead 'fellow' was in Heaven already, or waiting in Purgatory. Katherine, found this most unsatisfactory and unsettling; it was the difference, she said, between 'Henry landing in Australia & enjoying the kangaroos, & Henry still tossed on unknown seas'.

I can see the pair of them in my mind's eye, strolling through the fields of Paradise, enjoying the kangaroos.

Acknowledgements

When compressing two such large lives and so many works into such a small book for general readers, much must be left out. Lacking space for footnotes, I can only refer scholars to the extensive bibliography and recommend them to investigate the treasure trove of diaries for themselves. Among Michael Field scholars I am particularly grateful to Mary Sturgeon, J.G. Paul Delaney and Jerusha Hull McCormack for their work on which I have relied greatly.

I thank the following for permissions kindly granted:

Leonie Sturge-Moore and Charmian O'Neil (the copyright holders) and the Bodleian Library, University of Oxford (the owner), for Katherine Bradley's 1867-8 diary, shelfmark MS. Eng. misc. e. 336.

Leonie Sturge-Moore and Charmian O'Neil (the copyright holders) and the British Library (the owner) for the Michael Field and Ricketts and Shannon MSS detailed in the bibliography.

Bibliography

Works of Michael Field

By Katherine Bradley writing as 'Arran Leigh':
The New Minnesinger and Other Poems (London: Longman, Green & Co., 1875)

By Katherine Bradley and Edith Cooper writing as 'Arran and Isla Leigh':
Bellerophôn (London: C. Kegan Paul & Co., 1881)

By Katherine Bradley and Edith Cooper writing as 'Michael Field':
Callirrhoë and Fair Rosamund (London: George Bell & Sons, and Clifton: J. Baker and Son, 1884)
The Father's Tragedy, William Rufits and Loyalty or Love? (London: George Bell & Sons, and Clifton: J. Baker and Son, 1885)
Brutus Ultor (London: J. Baker and Son, 1886)
Canute the Great and The Cup of Water (London: George Bell & Sons, 1887)
Long Ago (London: George Bell & Sons, 1889)
The Tragic Mary (London: George Bell & Co., 1890)
Stephania: A Trialogue (London: Elkin Mathews and John Lane, 1892)
Sight and Song (London: Elkin Mathews and John Lane, 1892)
Underneath the Bough: A Book of Verses (London: George Bell & Sons, first edition, Spring 1893; 'revised and decreased edition', Autumn 1893)
A Question of Memory (London: Elkin Mathews and John Lane, 1893)
Equal Love in The Pageant, ed. by Charles Shannon and J. W. G. White (London: 1896 [1895]), pp.189–224
Attila, my Attila! (London: Elkin Mathews, 1896 [1895])
Fair Rosamund (second edition; London: Hacon & Ricketts at the Sign

of the Dial, 1897)
The World at Auction (London: The Vale Press, 1898)
Underneath the Bough [expanded edition] (Portland, Maine: 1898)
Anna Ruina (London: David Nutt, 1899)
Noontide Branches: A Small Sylvan Drama, Interspersed with Songs and Invocations (Oxford: H. Daniel, 1899) *The Race of Leaves* (London: The Vale Press, 1901)
Julia Domna (London: The Vale Press, 1903)

By Katherine Bradley and Edith Cooper writing anonymously:
Borgia: A Period Play (London: A. H. Bullen, 1905)

By Katherine Bradley and Edith Cooper writing as 'the author of Borgia':
Queen Mariamne (London: Sidgwick and Jackson, 1908)
The Tragedy of Pardon and Diane (London: Sidgwick and Jackson, 1911)
The Accuser, Tristan de Leonois and A Messiah (London: Sidgwick and Jackson, 1911)

By Katherine Bradley and Edith Cooper writing as 'Michael Field':
Wild Honey from Various Thyme (London: T. Fisher Unwin, 1908)
Poems of Adoration (London and Edinburgh: Sands & Co., 1912)
Mystic Trees (London: Eveleigh Nash, 1913)
Whym Chow: Flame of Love (London: Eragny Press, 1914)
Dedicated: An Early Work of Michael Field (London: George Bell & Sons, 1914)
Deirdre, A Question of Memory [revised edition] and *Ras Byzance* (London: The Poetry Bookshop, 1918)
In the Name of Time (London: The Poetry Bookshop, 1919)
A Selection from the Poems of Michael Field, with a preface by T. Sturge Moore [who trimmed many of the poems] (London: The Poetry Bookshop, 1923)
The Wattlefold: Unpublished Poems, collected by Emily C. Fortey, preface by V. McNabb (Oxford: Basil Blackwell, 1930)
Works and Days: From the foumal of Michael Field (London: John Murray, 1933), ed. by T. and D.C. Sturge Moore, with an introduction by Sir William Rothenstein
Sight and Song and Underneath the Bough (Oxford: Woodstock, 1993)

English Verse Drama, full-text database (Chadwyck-Healey), includes 26 of Michael Field's plays.

English Poetry, full-text database (Chadwyck-Healey), includes 565 of Michael Field's poems.

Planned, Unfinished or Unpublished Works
(The whereabouts of any surviving manuscripts are not known.)

Effigies, a collection of early prose pieces by Edith.
Old Wine in New Bottles, a contemporary prose play by Edith, 1892.
Modem Virtue, a prose play, begun by 1893.
Comeus, a prose play about living through children, begun 1893.
Croysis, inspired by Edith's feelings for BB, 1893.
A modern prose play about a doctor and a girl whose mother was mad, possibly called *A Turn of the Tide*, 1894–5.
Quits, a play Edith was working on, 1894.
Omens, 1894.
For That Moment Only, a collection of Edith 's prose pieces, 1894.
A Celtic play based on Cuchulainn's love affair with Farm, conceived in 1895.
A play by Katherine about Scottish witches, begun 1895.
Io Bacchel, a dramatic poem by Edith, 1895–9.
Anthony Derivian or *The Abbot of Glastonbury*, a play planned 1896.
The Loves of Alexander and the Moon, a play planned by Edith, 1896.
John Tzimisces, a Byzantine play planned by Edith, 1896.
Zeus in Crete, a long poem about early religion, planned 1900.
The Fair Miracle, a play about a female equivalent of Carloman from *In the Name of Time*, planned 1896, begun by Katherine 1900.
A '*Tetralogy of Beauty*', planned 1901, to be made up of *Deirdre, Mary of Scotland* (quite different to *The Tragic Mary*), a third play about Iseult of Cornwall, and one about Helen of Troy.
The Temple, a play about characters called Sigismondo Malatesta and Isotta, planned by Edith, 1903.
A trilogy about Elizabeth I (Elizabeth as Princess, Elizabeth and Mary Smart, and an Elizabeth and Essex play called *Rebellion*) planned by Katherine, 1903.
Cesar's Tower, or *Caesar Dominator*, an Italian play by Edith, 1904.
A Flower of Wrath, a play based on a story of Boccaccio's, written 1906.
A play about Caligula, begun 1907.
A play for marionettes, planned by Edith, 1912.
God's Myrtle Pot, a book by Edith on God's love, 1912.

Revised versions of *The Cup of Water* and *The Tragic Mary*.

Manuscripts

In the Bodleian Library:
MS. Engl. misc. e. 336 (KB's diary, July 1867 – May 1868)
In the British Library:
Michael Field papers: Add. MSS 45851–45856 (MF correspondence, 1871–1911); 46776 (KB's Paris diary, October 1868 – February 1869); 46777 (MF diaries, entitled '*Works and Days*', 1888 – 1889); 46778 (1890); 46779 (1891); 46780 (1892); 46781 (1893); 46782 (1894); 46783 (1895 Vol. I); 46784 (1895 Vol. II); 46785 (1896); 46786 (1897); 46787 (1898); 46788 (1899); 46789 (1900); 46790 (1901); 46791 (1902); 46792 (1903); 46793 (1904); 46794 (1905); 46795 (1906); 46796 (1907 Vol. I); 46797 (1907 Vol. II); 46798 (1908); 46799 (1909); 46800 (1910); 46801 (1911); 46802 (1912); 46803 (1913); 46804.a (1914); 46804.b.i (loose material from 1868 to 1899); 46804.b.ii (loose material from 1899 to 1914).

Ricketts and Shannon papers: Add. MSS 50548 (CR's letters); 51724 (CR's draft writings); 52747 (CR's letters); 58085 (CR's letters to CS, 1900–31); 58086 (CR's letters to T. Sturge Moore, 1891–1931); 58087 (correspondence of CR and CS, mostly with MF, 1892 – 1902); 58088 (1903 – 1905); 58089 (1906 – 1914); 58092–58093 (CR's draft writings); 58094–58097 (CR's travel journals); 58098–58109 (CR's diaries 1900–06, 1914–18); 58110–58118 (CS's diaries, 1898–1908). T. Sturge Moore, annotated typed copies of Ricketts and Shannon papers. Add. MSS 61713–61724.

Studies of Michael Field

Biederstedt, Joan, '*The Poetic Plays of Michael Field*', Phd Thesis, Loyola University of Chicago, 1964
Ireland, Kenneth R., '*Sight and Song: A Study of the Interrelations between Painting and Poetry*', Victorian Poetry, 15: 1 (1977), 9–20
Knittel, Janna Marie, '*Convention and Counterpoint: Nineteenth-Century Women's Poetic Language*' [Dickinson, Harper, Rossetti, Field, Guiney, Mew], Phd Thesis, University of Oregon, 1995
Laird, Holly, '*Contradictory Legacies: Michael Field and Feminist Restoration*', Victorian Poetry, 33: 1 (1995), 111–28
Leighton, Angela, *Victorian Women Poets*, Harvester, Hemel Hempstead, 1992, chapter on Michael Field pp. 202–43
Locard, Henri, '*Le Journal d'Edmond et Jules de Goncourt et Works and*

Days de 'Michael Field',' Confluents (1976), 53–77

Locard, Henri, 'Michael Field and Music', Confluents (1977), 69–77

Locard, Henri, 'Michael Field et la 'lecture' de Verlaine à Barnard's Inn', Confluents (1975), 91–101

Locard, Henri, 'Works and Days: The Journals of "Michael Field",' Journal of the Eighteen Nineties Society, 10 (1979), 1–9

McDonald, Jan, ' "Disillusioned Bards and Despised Bohemians": Michael Field's A Question of Memory at the Independent Theatre Society', Theatre NoteBook, 31: 2 (1977), 18–29

Madden, Norman Edward, 'Lyric Transvestism: Gender and Voice in Modernist Literature' [Barnes, Clarke, Eliot, Field, Mew], PhD Thesis, University of Texas at Austin, 1994

Moriarty, David. J, ' "Michael Field" (Edith Cooper and Katherine Bradley) and Their Male Critics,', in Nineteenth-Century Women Writers of the English-Speaking World, ed. by Rhoda B. Nathan (Westwood, CT: Greenwood Press, 1986), pp. 121–42

Pearsall Smith, Logan, Reperusals and Re-collections (London: Constable, 1936), chapter on Michael Field [written 1924], pp. 85–97

Prins, Yopie, 'A Metaphorical Field: Katherine Bradley and Edith Cooper', Victorian Poetry, 33: 1 (1995), 129–48

Prins, Yopie, 'Sappho Doubled: Michael Field', Yale Journal of Criticism, 8: 1 (1995), 165–86

Psomiades, Kathy Alexis, 'Subtly of Herself Contemplative: Women, Poets, and British Aestheticism' [Rossetti, Field], Phd Thesis, Yale University, 1990

Ricketts, Charles, Michael Field [an essay], ed. by Paul Delaney (Edinburgh: Tragara Press, 1976)

Sturgeon, Mary, Michael Field (London: Harrap, 1922)

White, Chris, ' "Poets and Lovers Ever More": Interpreting Female Love in the Poetry and Journals of Michael Field', Textual Practice, 4 (1990), 197–212

White, Chris, The One Woman (in virgin haunts of poesie): Michael Field's Sapphic symbolism', in Volcanoes and Pearl Divers: Essays in Lesbian Feminist Studies, ed. by Suzanne Raitt (London: Onlywomen, 1995), pp. 74–102

Other Sources
Abse, Joan, John Ruskin: The Passionate Moralist (London: Quartet Books, 1980)

Beckson, Karl, and John M. Munro, ed. *Arthur Symons: Selected Letters, 1880–1935* (London: Macmillan, 1989)

Beckson, Karl, *Arthur Symons: A Life* (Oxford: Clarendon Press, 1987)

Besant, Walter, 'On Literary Collaboration', *The New Review*, 6 (1892), 200–9

Casal, Mary, *The Stone Wall: An Autobiography* (Chicago: Eyncourt Press, 1930)

Christian, John, ed. *The Last Romantics* (London: Lund Humphries, 1985)

Cline, C.L., ed. *The Letters of George Meredith*, 3 vols (Oxford: Clarendon Press, 1970)

Darracott, Joseph, *The World of Charles Ricketts* (London: Eyre Methuen, 1980)

Delaney, J. G. Paul, and Stephen Calloway, ed. *Charles Ricketts and Charles Shannon: An Aesthetic Partnership* (Twickenham: Orleans House Gallery, 1979)

Delaney, J. G. Paul, *Charles Ricketts: A Biography* (Oxford: Clarendon Press, 1990)

Delaney, J. G. Paul, ed. *Letters from Charles Ricketts to 'Michael Field'* (1903–1913) (Edinburgh: Tragary Press, 1981)

Delaney, J. G. Paul, ed. *Some Letters from Charles Ricketts and Charles Shannon to 'Michael Field'* (1894–1902) (Edinburgh: Tragara Press, 1979)

Delaney, J. G. Paul, ed. *The Lithographs of Charles Shannon 1863 – 1937* (London: Taranman, 1978)

Donoghue, Emma, ed. *What Sappho Would Have Said: Four Centuries of Love Poems Between Women* (London: Harmish Hamilton, 1997), US title *Poems Between Women: Four Centuries of Love, Romantic Friendship and Desire* (New York: Columbia University Press, 1997)

Doughty, Frances, 'Lesbian Biography, Biography of Lesbians', in *Lesbian Studies: Present and Future*, ed. by Margaret Cruikshank (Old Westbury, NY: The Feminist Press, 1982), pp. 122–27

Ellis, Havelock, *Studies in the Psychology of Sex: Sexual Inversion* (London, University Press, Watford, 1897)

Faderman, Lillian, 'Who Hid Lesbian History?', in *Cruikshank*, op cit, pp. 115–21

Faderman, Lillian, ed. *Chloe Plus Olivia: An Anthology of Lesbian Literature from the Seventeenth Century to the Present* (New York: Viking, 1994)

Faderman, Lillian, *Surpassing the Love of Men* (New York: William Morrow, 1981)

Foster, Jeannette H., *Sex Variant Women in Literature* [1956] (Tallahassee, Fl.: Naiad, 1985)

Gardner, Burdett, *The Lesbian Imagination* (Victorian Style): *A Psychological and Critical Study of 'Vernon Lee'* [a 1952 dissertation] (New York and London: Garland, 1987)

Griffin, Gabriele, *Heavenly Love? Lesbian Images in Twentieth-Century Women's Writing* (Manchester and New York: Manchester University Press, 1993)

Grosskurth, Phyllis, *Havelock Ellis: A Biography* (London: Allen Lane, 1980)

Hughes, W. R., *Constance Naden* (London: 1890)

Johnson, Lionel, 'Michael Field', in Alfred H. Miles, ed. *The Poets and Poetry of the Nineteenth Century* (London: Hutchinson & Co., 1891), Vol. 10

Koestenbaum, Wayne, *Double Talk: The Erotics of Male Literary Collaboration* (New York and London: Roudedge, 1989)

Krishnamurti, G, ed. *Women Writers of the 1890s*, introduced by Margaret Drabble (London: Henry Sotheran Ltd, 1991)

Legge, Sylvia, *Affectionate Cousins: T. Sturge Moore and Marie Appia* (Oxford: Oxford University Press, 1980)

Leighton, Angela, and Margaret Reynolds, ed. *Victorian Women Poets: An Anthology* (Oxford: Blackwell, 1995)

McCormack, Jerusha Hull, *John Gray: Poet, Dandy, and Priest* (Hanover and London: Brandeis University Press, 1991)

Parker, Stephen, *Informal Marriage, Cohabitation and the Law*, 1750–1989 (London: Macmillan, 1990)

Phillips, Ann, ed. *A Newnham Anthology*, (Cambridge: Cambridge University Press, 1979)

Ricketts, Charles, *Self-Portrait Taken from the Letters and Journals of Charles Ricketts*, R.A., collected and compiled by T. Sturge Moore, ed. by Cecil Lewis (London: Peter Davies, 1939)

Robinson, Hilary, *Somerville & Ross: A Critical Appreciation* (Dublin: Gill and Macmillan, 1980)

Rothenstein, William, *Men and Memories: Recollections 1872–1938* (London: Chatto & Windus, 1978)

Samuels, Ernest, *Bernard Berenson: The Making of a Connoisseur* (London: Harvard University Press, 1979)

Secrest, Meryle, *Being Bernard Berenson: A Biography* (London: Weidenfeld & Nicolson, 1980)

Sewell, Brocard, *In the Dorian Mode: A Life of John Gray, 1866–1934* (Cornwall: Tabb House, 1983)

Smith II, Philip E., and Susan Harris Smith, 'Constance Naden: Late Victorian Feminist Poet and Philosopher', *Victorian Peary 15:* 4 (Winter 1977), 367–70

Stillinger, Jack, *Multiple Authorship & The Myth of Solitary Genius* (New York and Oxford: Oxford University Press, 1991)

Strachey, Barbara and Jayne Samuels, ed. *Mary Berenson: A Self-Portrait from her Letters and Diaries* (London: Victor Gollancz, 1983)

Swinburne, Algernon, *Letters*, ed. by C. Y. Lang, 6 vols (New Haven: Yale University Press, 1958–62)

Symons, Arthur, ed. *An Anthology of 'Nineties Verse* (London: E. Mathews and Marrot, 1928), poems by Michael Field pp. 56–70

Vicinus, Martha, 'The Adolescent Boy: Fin de Siècle Femme Fatale?', *Journal of the History of Sexuality*, 5: 1 (July 1994), 90–114

Wang, Shou-ren, *The Theatre of the Mind: A Study of Unacted Drama in Nineteenth-Century England* (London: Macmillan, 1990)

Wharton, Henry Thornton, *Sappho: A Memoir and Translation* (London: 1885)

Williams, David, *George Meredith: His Life and Lost Love* (London: Hamish Hamilton, 1977)

Yeats, W.B., *The Oxford Book of Modern Verse, 1892–1935* (Oxford: Clarendon Press, 1936)

www.ingramcontent.com/pod-product-compliance
Ingram Content Group UK Ltd.
Pitfield, Milton Keynes, MK11 3LW, UK
UKHW010618150625
459569UK00006BA/14